THE HISTORY OF A
GREAT MOTORCYCLE

By the same author:
      British Sports Cars
      500 cc Racing
      Formula 2
      Boys' Book of Motoring Sport
      World Championship

THE HISTORY OF A GREAT MOTORCYCLE
GREGOR GRANT

PSL

Patrick Stephens, London

First published – October 1969

SBN 85059 038 8

Set in 10 on 11 pt Times Roman type.
Printed in Great Britain for Patrick Stephens Ltd,
9 Ely Place, London EC1,
by Blackfriars Press Ltd, Leicester
and bound by Hunter & Foulis Ltd, Edinburgh.

Foreword by John Surtees

ALTHOUGH MY LIFE is now devoted to racing cars, I still have a great affection for the two-wheeler world, and for all those connected with it. There are all too few books on motorcycles, as distinct from motorcycling, and I must say that I cannot recall having seen one which deals with a specific make, unless it was a handbook. I am sure many bike enthusiasts will be grateful to my friend Gregor Grant for chronicling the history of AJS, a marque which has always had the closest possible connection with motorcycle sport. In fact, had I not required every available bit of capital several years ago for a business venture, I might well have been racing my own particular version, making use of that splendid power unit, the overhead camshaft 7R 'Boys' Racer'. I did go as far as to build one, and I felt that it was a most competitive '350'. However, I had to sell it, and that bike eventually became the Arter-AJS, which was raced so successfully by Mike Duff.

I well recall the 'Porcupine', which, had ample funds been available and less politics existed at Plumstead in those days, could have made a much greater impact than was the case. The factory was not exactly blessed with the best of luck when it raced them—particularly over in the Island. Many of the 7Rs were very competitive, and I remember Bob McIntyre giving John Hartle and me a run for our money when he hung on to our MV-Agustus in the 1959 'Junior'. Also I had great trouble holding Alan Shepherd in the 1960 Ulster Grand Prix, for his 7R was every bit as quick as my MV, and he shadowed me till the camshaft chain broke, a thing which the AJS people maintained had never happened before. The Italians took a good deal of convincing that Alan's engine dimensions were strictly legal—which they were!

Maybe one day the famous initials will be back in big-time racing. AJS have always built good machines, and when you think about it, it is seven years since 7Rs were made, and they still earn their keep, and fetch remarkably high prices. As for an original 'big port' of the 1920s, that must be worth a lot of money, and at a guess there aren't many of these being offered around!

Anyway, with this book on my shelves, I feel that I shall know more about AJS than I ever did before.

Illustrations

Diagrams in Text

Contents

AJS Highlights in brief

1897 First Stevens motorcycle produced.

1909 First AJS motorcycles marketed.

1911 First entry in TT races.

1914 Victory in Junior TT. A. J. Stevens and Co (1914) Ltd formed. Works moved from Wednesfield to Graiseley House, Wolverhampton. Winner Brooklands Junior TT.

1920 Overhead valve machine introduced. Victory in Junior TT. First 350 cc machine to attain 80 mph. Five Gold Medals in ACU English Six Days Trial.

1921 Howard Davies wins Senior TT on '350'. AJS first, second and third in Junior TT.

1922 First and second in Junior TT. 'Big port' appears.

1923 'Big port' in production.

1924 First 60 mph lap in Junior TT by Jimmy Simpson. Simpson 350 cc European champion.

1926 First 70 mph lap in Senior TT by Jimmy Simpson.

Rex Adams wins 350 cc Amateur TT.

1927 Overhead camshaft machine appears in Isle of Man.

1928 Experimental four-cylinder machine constructed.

1929 AJS machines hold 117 world records. Overhead camshaft machine in production.

1930 Jimmy Guthrie wins Lightweight TT. Transverse twin '500' in production.

1931 A. J. Stevens and Co (1914) Ltd taken over by H. Collier and Sons Ltd. Factory moved to Plumstead, in South East London.

1933 Overhead camshaft model re-introduced.

1935 Four-cylinder machine exhibited at Olympia motorcycle show.

1936 AJS air-cooled 'fours' raced in Senior TT.

1937 Superchargers fitted to 'fours'.

1938 Colliers incorporated in Associated Motorcycles Ltd, ie, Norton, AJS, Matchless, James and Francis-Barnett. 'Fours' now water-cooled, and, riding one, Rusk does first 100 mph lap in Ulster GP.

1947 'Porcupines' appear in Senior TT. Details of 7R announced. Hugh Viney wins Scottish Six Days Trial.

1948 Hugh Viney wins Scottish Six Days Trial.

1949 Hugh Viney wins Scottish Six Days Trial.

1950 Don Crossley (7R) wins Junior Manx GP.

1951 Robin Sherry (7R) wins Junior Manx GP.

1952 Bob McIntyre, Harold Clark and Derek Farrant (7Rs) first, second and third in Junior Manx TT.

1953 Hugh Viney wins Scottish Six Days Trial. AJS take manufacturers' award.

1954 Rod Coleman (Triple-knocker) wins Junior TT. Derek Ennett (7R) wins Manx Junior GP. AJS takes manufacturers' award in Scottish Six Days Trial.

1955 AJS takes manufacturers' award in Scottish Six Days Trial.

1956 Gordon Jackson wins Scottish Six Days Trial. Manufacturers' award won by AJS.

1958 Gordon Jackson wins Scottish Six Days Trial. Alan Shepherd (7R) wins Junior Manx GP.

1960 Gordon Jackson wins Scottish Six Days Trial.

1961 Gordon Jackson wins Scottish Six Days Trial. Frank Reynolds, Robin Dawson and A. Newstead (7Rs) first, second and third in Junior Manx GP.

1962 Robin Dawson and Peter Darvill (7Rs) first and second in Junior Manx GP. 7R production ceases.

1963 Peter Darvill, Alan Hunter and Selwyn Griffiths (7Rs) first, second and third in Junior Manx GP.

1965 Malcolm Uphill (7R) wins Junior Manx GP.

1966 Peter Inchley finishes third in Lightweight TT on Villiers Starmaker Special. Norton Villiers acquire five marques, including AJS, from the AMC Receiver.

1967 Prototype AJS Y4 Scrambler built.

1968 Malcolm Davis (Y4) wins 250 cc British Motocross Championship.

1969 First Y4s exported. Factory moves to Andover, Hants. New 246 cc 37A-T trials machine introduced. USA corporation formed on West Coast.

Introduction by Dennis Poore
Chairman of Norton Villiers Limited

FROM THE EARLIEST machines made at the turn of the century to the legendary successes of the Nortons in the Isle of Man in the mid-'fifties, British motorcycles have enjoyed a pre-eminent place and have for ever been in the forefront of the news. However, international agreements called 'GATT', which were then introduced to encourage world trade, opened the floodgates of competition on the British home market and the story changed to one of commercial struggle. The years of lotus-eating protectionism following World War II were now exacting their toll. Engineering expenditure had to be reduced when the dire need was to do just the opposite. The lead of the British manufacturers, particularly in the smaller machines, was taken over by others.

By 1961 the picture was bleak indeed. Associated Motorcycles Limited, the once proud home of so many famous marques, was languishing under a heavy burden of debt. The Villiers Engineering Company Limited, which had been the foremost supplier of small petrol engines for industrial and motorcycle use since most people could remember, was facing severe competition from American and Japanese imports; its profit and loss account was telling the inevitable tale.

What was to be done to rejuvenate this vital industry so that it could resume its proper place on the British scene? The answer proposed by my colleagues on the Manganese Bronze Holdings group board was a marriage of these two companies within our group. The financial implications were studied, obstacles overcome and the bold concept of this plan was started in 1962. By 1966 it had been consummated and Norton Villiers Limited was born.

Our plan for recovery is based on a new engineering approach, to be applied in the first instance to the world-famous Norton and AJS. The first fruits of this policy can be found in the Norton Commando and in the AJS 'Y' Series Scramblers.

A history of AJS has long been overdue and we should all be grateful to Gregor Grant for the record he has now produced, which spans three-quarters of a century, and for his reminder of the achievements and traditions of a marque which will surely never die. We at Norton Villiers Limited intend that the new breed of AJS will enhance these traditions established so long ago by those dedicated enthusiasts, the Stevens brothers, whose initiative and foresight first created the demand for lightweight sporting machines and whose initials remain our badge.

Acknowledgements

I AM MOST GRATEFUL for the assistance given to me in the preparation of this book by Harry Louis, renowned editor-in-chief of 'Motor Cycle' and his staff at Dorset House; to eminent motor-cycling journalist Peter Arnold for so painstakingly reading the typescript and proofs, only a few weeks before he was tragically killed in a road accident; to that great rider and personality Jock West, who was so closely involved with the 'Porcupines' and 'Boys' Racers'; to Peter Inchley, the man behind the modern Y4 AJS; to curator Michael Ware of the Montagu Museum, Beaulieu; to Harry Downing and Lou Ellis of Shell-Mex and BP for digging up records of the past; and to Peter Howdle of 'Motor Cycle News' for finding some splendid pictures. My thanks are also due to Dennis Poore, chairman of Norton Villiers, for giving me the opportunity to do something that I have really enjoyed.

Gregor Grant.

Chapter 1

a marque is born

THE STEVENS BROTHERS—Harry, George, Jack and Joe—were the sons of an engineering black-smith, Joe Stevens, who lived and worked at Wednesfield, near Wolverhampton. There was a fifth son, Billy, but he was not concerned directly with the subsequent activities of the family in the motorcycle world. Joe (Senior) was also by way of being a precision engineer and had a fine local reputation for high-grade work in his small factory, the Stevens Screw Co Ltd.

The father soon saw the possibilities of small-capacity, internal - combustion engines. He visualised portable equipment for wood-cutting, pumps and so on, using ic engines as the motive power. However, in the 1890s, there was no such thing as a proprietary engine; most of the pioneer manufacturers were building up engines mainly from imported De Dion bits and pieces. However, by 1897, several American companies had begun to construct power-units, and Joe (Senior) managed to acquire a small Mitchell single-cylinder four-stroke engine from the USA.

It was probably the Werner which inspired the Stevens family with the idea of building a complete motorcycle. When what is generally acknowledged to have been the first Stevens motorcycle appeared in 1897, it followed the Werner layout, in that the Mitchell engine was mounted on the front down-tube of a bicycle frame, with a slab-shaped petrol tank suspended from the cross-bar. However, un-like the front-drive Werner, the Stevens drove the rear wheel, the belt passing over an intermediate pulley.

During the next decade, the Stevens Screw Co Ltd was engaged on engine production, starting off with a better-built version of the Mitchell. The power-units were made by the four sons, working under the direction of their father. The Stevens engine soon achieved a reputation for durability, which commended the make to Werner and Wolf, two of the most prominent motorcycle makers at the turn of the century. The early Stevens had automatic valves, trembler ignition and a surface carburettor.

In Edwardian days, the Stevens family built a variety of engines, including a vertical twin for Wolf, and a wide-angle Vee-twin for Clyno. They had also gone into the frame business, securing quite a number of useful contracts. In 1905, the company was also building a vertical-twin, water-cooled engine, which was fitted in one or two three-wheelers of the period. By 1910, Stevens had gone over to mechanically operated valves, and were now seriously thinking of continuing the dream of 1897—producing motorcycles.

Jack was a great believer in motorcycling sport as a means of development, and for some time he and his brothers had been riding in trials and speed events on various machines, including Wolf, fitted with Stevens engines. This machine was built by the Wearwell Cycle Co Ltd, and one of their motorcycles, fitted with a Stevens engine, was awarded a special ACU certificate in 1909 for an observed 24-hours non-stop run.

When the ACU divided the Tourist Trophy race into events for Junior and Senior machines, Jack decided to enter for the former, which was open to motorcycles of up to 300 cc. The name AJS was chosen for the new make, this being the result of a disinclination to use Stevens, because it was associated with the manufacture of proprietary engines. The initials came about because the eldest brother, Albert John (Jack) was the only one who had a middle initial.

The Stevens side-valve engine was a most successful little unit and it was this that was fitted in the original AJS machines. It was of 298 cc (70 × 77.5 mm), very slightly larger than the proprietary ones which were of 292 cc (70 × 76 mm). A simple, diamond-type frame was used, with Druid-pattern, side-sprung forks, a two-speed counter-shaft gearbox and, for the TT, belt drive.

Jack was very satisfied that both of his machines had finished and, had he not taken a toss and been delayed by having to straighten his forks, he might well have been in the first half-dozen. As it was, private-owner J. D. Corke took 15th place, and Jack was 16th.

Busy with their new venture, the Stevens boys had no time to prepare machines for the 1912 TT. Customers were becoming more and more numerous for the handsome little lightweights, and the belt-drive of the 1911 TT machines had now given way to all-chain-drive.

AJS were again represented in the 1913 Junior TT with W. M. Heaton finishing tenth and Cyril Williams retiring. It seemed that nothing could defeat the twin-cylinder machines. Orthodoxy had triumphed over the freak motorcycles of earlier years. Gone were the front-engined machines, engines behind the riders, rotary-units with their immense gyroscopic problems and freaks such as the Eclipse XL-A11, which had a Vee-twin engine, on which either cylinder could be used separately if so desired.

If only AJS could break the stranglehold of the 'twins'! Since the introduction of the Mountain course in the Isle of Man, Vee-twins had won three races, parallel-twins two, and horizontally opposed twins, one. Also, every fastest lap had been achieved by a twin.

With the Junior engine limit raised to 350 cc, the 1914 TT AJS had a 349 cc unit, two-speed P & M primary drive, and two-speed additional countershaft gearbox, giving four speeds in all. This was truly a little masterpiece. In the search for reliability, cylinder and fins had been machined from a solid billet, and the piston was also machined from the solid. Months and months of exhaustive testing had resulted in an ideal cam contour and mods to valves and valve gear gave a perfectly safe rpm limit of 'five-thou'. The 298 cc 1911 TT engine would go up to 2,500 rpm, but beyond that all sorts of unfortunate things tended to occur.

The race resulted in a sweeping AJS victory, Eric Williams winning from Cyril Williams (no relation), and with Ajays also third, fourth and sixth. Almost overnight, AJS sales rocketed to such a degree that the old Screw Company's premises could not possibly cope and the new company, A. J. Stevens (1914) Ltd, moved into premises at Graiseley House, in the environs of Wolverhampton. Although the 2¾ hp model was most in demand, a 6 hp twin-cylinder machine was steadily gaining in popularity with sidecar enthusiasts. Cyril Williams easily won the 1914 Brooklands Junior TT, on the only AJS entered.

The World War caused motorcycle production to come to a standstill with Graiseley House going over to munitions, mainly components for the aircraft industry. During the war years a certain amount of development work continued, when priorities did not interfere, and when once again the factory was free to go into the business of motorcycle production in 1919, the 2¾ hp and 6 hp machines were already much-improved from the 1914-15 models.

The story of the phenomenal little ohv '350' is told elsewhere, and three successive Junior victories in 1920, 1921 and 1922 enhanced the prestige of AJS immeasurably. Jack's enterprise in entering the 1911 TT had certainly paid dividends, winning

the 1914 event, and then dominating the three post-war races.

One could truthfully say that the 1920 overhead valve AJS completely altered the picture, in so far as lightweight, sporting solos were concerned. With the valves inclined in the head at a wide angle, a true hemispherical combustion shape was the result (a theory that had been vindicated in no uncertain manner by Peugeot, with their pre-war, Henry-designed, twin-ohc car racing engines).

Each year, the AJS business expanded. Innumerable world records were broken at Brooklands, Montlhéry and Arpajon. The 'big port' gave the clubman an ideal mount for every possible type of speed event and the normal road machines had established themselves as quality products, backed by first-class engineering.

The introduction of the overhead camshaft model in 1927 was another landmark in AJS history. Chain-drive for valve operation was quite an innovation in the motorcycle world and was proved to be completely reliable. In 1930, a 250 cc version, with Jimmy Guthrie in the saddle, won the Lightweight TT.

Yet the fortunes of the Stevens brothers were none too rosy. By this time, the company was in business in a big way. Quite apart from motorcycles, the concern was building its own sidecars and a fine 10 hp motor-car was being produced. In addition, Harry had gone into the radio business and the company had also entered the commercial vehicle field. Capital was being swallowed up, and the chain-reaction which followed the Wall Street crash in 1929 reached out to Europe. Unemployment figures rose and the sales of motorcycles dropped because people just did not have the money to spend. As expenditure went up, income dropped and by early 1931 A. J. Stevens and Co Ltd was in such a precarious state that the brothers had no option but to go into liquidation.

It seemed likely that the great name of AJS would follow so many makes into oblivion—ABC, BAT, Beardmore, Humber, Werner, Wearwell, Zenith—these, and many more had gone.

BSA made overtures, but these came to naught. Then into the breach stepped H. Collier and Sons Ltd, makers of the Matchless. The brothers Harry and Charlie acquired the entire assets of AJS, and moved the factory from Graiseley House to Plumstead, Woolwich. For a year or so the Stevens family produced a 250 cc machine under their own name and carried on with the marketing of the AJS car, but these enterprises did not survive for very long.

Colliers speedily adopted a rationalisation policy, producing AJS models which were similar to those of Matchless origin, but continuing the big-twin, sidecar model. Nevertheless they did attempt to retain the AJS individuality which was emphasised when the 'cammy' AJS was re-introduced in 1933. It was realised that the name AJS, with its history of competition successes, was well worth publicising. In 1935 a more progressive policy was adopted when a highly exciting four-cylinder AJS was exhibited at the Olympia motorcycle show. It was never put into production but became the basis of racing machines which are fully described in another chapter.

Back in 1929, George Stevens had produced an experimental 'in-line four', of which five were known to have been completed. I believe one still survives today, the machine which George himself used to ride with a sidecar attached.

Of 660 cc, the engine was a monobloc iron casting with deep horizontal finning. The overhead valves were operated by four sets of push-rods, and the two inside pistons rose together. A single Amal carburettor was employed and a four-speed AJS gearbox was in unit with the engine. The frame was merely a lengthened version of the standard 500 cc machine which produced an inordinately long wheelbase. Although it worked quite well as a sidecar outfit, from all accounts it was a pig to ride solo.

The power-unit was remarkably smooth and extremely quiet for an air-cooled 'four'. However, heavy oil consumption was something that the AJS technicians could not cure and the scheme was abandoned—probably to the great relief of George's brothers.

The transverse Vee-twin of 1932 had immense possibilities, but the Colliers took a good look at the cost of recovering the tooling expenses and very few of these machines were completed after the take-over.

In 1938, H. Collier and Sons Ltd were absorbed in Associated Motor Cycles Ltd. Harry Collier, the elder brother, died in 1944, but Charlie saw the share capital more than double by 1947. AMC took over Francis-Barnett, James and Norton, in August 1947, November 1950 and November 1953, but AJS and Matchless continued to be built at Plumstead. During the years from 1947 to 1952, AJS machines had a wonderful record of successes in trials, the 350 cc 16MC becoming as famous as had the 'big port' and the 'cammy' in the past. The introduction of the 7R, or 'Boys' Racer' was yet another successful venture. It was a great pity that the ingenious twin-cylinder 'Porcupines' did not meet with the success they deserved in the TT.

It was planned thinking that caused these beautifully-made machines to be built, for AMC did realise that the day of the specially-designed racing 'multis' was on the way and that it was up to a British manufacturer to face the coming threat from the continent of Europe.

By the 1960s, AMC were in a none too healthy state. The influx of Japanese-built machines had hit the industry hard and no manufacturer was in a position to construct the extremely expensive machines essential to win the TT or foreign Grands Prix.

Nowadays, the fortunes of AJS are bound up with the powerful Norton Villiers concern, resulting in an extremely potent scrambler, the Y4. An out-and-out competition '250', it has been ridden with outstanding success in national and international events, notably by Malcolm Davies. It is the first AJS to have a two-stroke engine, this being developed from an original Villiers design by Peter Inchley, who had been responsible for the Starmaker-Villiers which did so well in the 1966 Lightweight TT.

Norton, Matchless and AJS machines will be manufactured in the modern new NV factory at Andover, the old Plumstead buildings having passed into the hands of the Greater London Council.

As a competition machine, the 250 cc AJS will find plenty of customers. The engineering standards are very high indeed and, with the ever-increasing interest in motocross events all over the world, Norton Villiers have done a wise thing in concentrating on such a delightful little machine.

The more one thinks about it, the achievements of AJS are almost a complete history of motorcycling, with a pedigree going as far back as 1897, when old Joe Stevens acquired that original single-cylinder engine and fired his sons with the ambition one day to build their own motorcycles.

In the following chapters, I hope to provide the full story of the marque: the machines, the men who rode them, and the men who made them. With such a glorious past as AJS has, the future must be full of promise, and I believe that I can say with every conviction that, during the next few years, the famous initials will make just as strong an impact as on that famous June day, so many years ago, when the products of the Stevens family completely swept the board in the Isle of Man Junior TT.

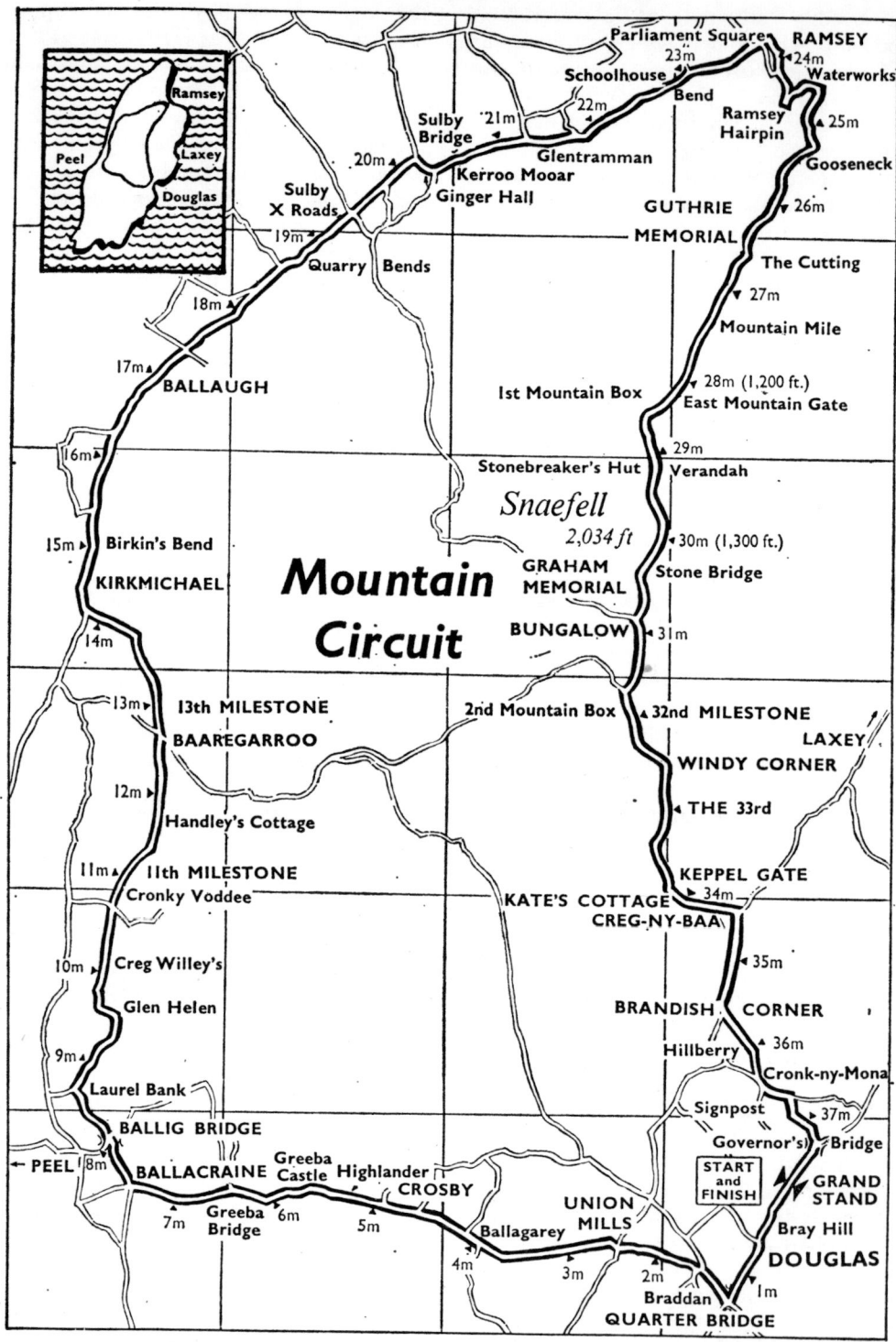

The Isle of Man Mountain Circuit, 37¾ miles of the toughest going in motorcycle racing. It was in the TT races that the marque AJS was nurtured, winning the Junior event in successive years, 1914, 1920, 1921 and 1922. There were, of course, no races during the First World War.   Shell-Mex-BP.

14

Chapter 2

AJS and the tourist trophy

WITH MEMORIES OF the 1914 success in the Isle of Man, Jack Stevens and his brothers went to work immediately after the cessation of hostilities on their 'secret weapon'. This was an overhead valve engine with both valves inclined in the head—a completely new departure for a British motorcycle manufacturer. By the time the TT races were revived in 1920, the new ohv AJS was ready. When it arrived in Douglas, rivals swarmed all over it, shaken to learn that the engine was giving 10 bhp —a prodigious output for 350 cc in those days. Also, the pre-war transmission had been replaced by an ingenious 'two-plus-two' arrangement. (The machine is fully described in Chapter Three.)

A 250 cc category had been introduced to run concurrently with the '350s', and a total of 61 entries was received, of which seven were of 250 cc, including Gus Kuhn, Frank 'Pa' Applebee and R. O. Clark on new two-stroke Levises. The AJS challenge comprised Eric Williams, Cyril Williams, Howard Davies, H. V. Prescott, Ossie Wade and Tom Sheard, Wade's machine having a three-speed gearbox. The majority of the rival makes bore names that have long departed from the scene, such as Diamond, Ivy, Wooler, Aurore, Blackburne and New Comet.

Following practice, the general opinion was that the new Ajays would walk the Junior. They were faster than anything else, possessed immense acceleration, and had a fine team of riders. However, 'There's many a slip . . .' But, as expected, the others were very much also-rans, so much so that a dog-fight developed amongst the leading group of AJS riders. One by one they fell victim to mechanical troubles and the once formidable half-dozen was reduced to one machine, with Cyril Williams in the saddle.

Williams had an enormous lead over his nearest challenger, surprisingly enough, Clark's 250 cc Levis two-stroke. Spectators were saying: 'He could push it and still win'; and that was exactly what he had to do. At Keppel Gate, nearly four miles from the finish, the healthy crackle from the ohv engine turned into a series of bangs, and finally silence! Williams tried desperately to re-start, but the engine had about as much compression as a leaking balloon. There was nothing for it but 'Shanks' Pony'.

Meanwhile Clark was 'phut-phutting' his way

round, several miles behind. Maybe he was trying too hard, but near the 33rd Milestone he laid the model over at too great an angle, the outside flywheel clanged against the 'tarmac', and off he came a gigantic purler.

Meanwhile Williams soldiered on. As Jack Stevens, back at the pits in Glencrutchery Road, anxiously awaited news of his overdue rider, Cyril was pushing, coasting and foot-slogging his crippled machine, not realising the drama in the mountains, as Clark sought to unbend his damaged Levis, using tyre levers and bits of fence to straighten things out.

Then at the pits a tremendous cheer went up. Williams had been sighted at Governor's Bridge, pushing his AJS over the slight crest, and then vaulting into the saddle to paddle his way to the finish line. He was completely and utterly exhausted and scarcely heard the congratulations or felt the back-slapping.

So vast had been his lead when the last of his team-mates dropped out that, even allowing for his epic push, he had won by nearly ten minutes from the Blackburnes of Watson-Bourne and Holroyd. The unlucky Clark did eventually win the 250 cc race by an even greater margin from Kuhn and Applebee on the other two Levises. Incidentally, the registration number of Williams' machine was DA1082.

Naturally the Stevens brothers were highly delighted with the AJS victory but, at the same time, resented the somewhat pointless dog-fight which they reckoned may have aggravated the mechanical troubles. The failures appeared to be either due to loss of compression, or to difficulty with the four-speed transmission. As is related in Chapter Three, several modifications were carried out for the 1921 TT machines, including three-speed gearboxes and a patented copper-asbestos seal between cylinder head and barrel.

Howard Davies did a considerable amount of testing at Brooklands in preparation for the Isle of Man races, caning the little machine mercilessly. So much so, that the two hours record fell to him at 65.3 mph, which was pretty good going for a 350 cc machine, 48 years ago!

There was no shortage of bids to ride an Ajay in the 1921 races. Rumours flew around that Alec Bennett and Fred Dixon would be in the team, but when the entries were completed Jack Stevens had nominated Howard Davies, Eric Williams, Ossie Wade, Tom Sheard and H. F. Harris, who was the father of the noted sidecar racing exponent 'Pip' Harris. Private entries were in the hands of G. Kelly and V. Olsson. Davies was also entered in the Senior with the same machine, DA 6394. This decision was to have a remarkable sequel which will probably never be emulated in another Senior TT. However, let's start with the Junior race.

Eric Williams repeated his 1914 success by winning at 52.11 mph. Howard Davies would doubtless have won easily but for a last-lap puncture, which he repaired to finish second, setting the fastest lap at 55.15 mph. It was a sweeping victory for AJS, Manxman Tom Sheard taking third place, with privateer Kelly fourth and Wade and Harris sixth and eighth respectively. Only Olsson retired.

Now for the sensational Senior race, with Howard Davies, the pygmy amongst the giants. And giants they were, for they included Fred Dixon and Bert le Vack (Indians), Jack Emerson and Norman Black (Douglases), Tom de la Hay, George Dance and Alec Bennett (Sunbeams), Freddie Edmond (Triumph), Jimmy Shaw (Norton), Harry Langman (Scott), and many other top riders of the day.

Into the lead shot Fred Dixon on the red Indian, unique amongst TT riders as he favoured footboards instead of rests. For two laps the American machine held on, with Davies in second place, but following a spot of misfiring Dixon started to drop back. After a record lap at 56.40 mph, Edmond pushed his Triumph in front, relentlessly pursued by Davies and then by Dance and Bennett on their long-stroke Sunbeams. It was then George Dance's turn to lead, but to the amazement of the spectators Davies and his incredible AJS were not only holding second place but were actually closing up on the Sunbeam.

Alec Bennett assumed the leadership on lap four, but Davies snatched second place again. The Sunbeam rider tried all he knew, but on lap five the little Ajay had overtaken the 500 cc machine, and completed the circuit one second ahead. This was almost unbelievable! Giving away 150 cc and now starting to steam away from the '500s'—small wonder there were puzzled faces in the pits!

That sixth and final circuit is now history. The little AJS, with Davies riding a perfectly judged race, inexorably began to pile on a lead. Dixon pulled out all the stops, overtaking Bennett and also his team-mate le Vack. Edmond and his Triumph had dropped well back.

Back at the pits, just as he had done a year earlier, Jack Stevens awaited news of his rider. Past Ramsay safely, and Davies was still extending his lead. Then at the Gooseneck with about 12 miles to go, followed by the descent of the Mountain, the Verandah, the Bungalow, the 33rd Milestone, Kate's Cottage; all the familiar landmarks safely negotiated, and the AJS was still increasing its lead!

Recalling Williams' experience the year before, Jack kept his fingers crossed. The Ajay was now at Creg-ny-Baa; less than three miles to go, and Davies must have had something like a couple of minutes over Dixon! For the second year in succession, an AJS rider was cheered to the echo, but this time he swooped over the line with the little ohv engine sounding as healthy as it had done at the start. Howard Davies had achieved what was thought to be the impossible and, what was more, his 54.50 mph average was a record for the Isle of Man circuit. Fred Dixon duly took his second place, 2 minutes 13 seconds behind, with teammate Bert le Vack another 13 seconds adrift.

The unexpected defeat of the '500s' by a 350 cc machine had rather curious repercussions. Critics of the ACU reckoned that the victory was not due to the speed of the 350 cc AJS but to the fact that the circuit was unsuited to the more powerful 500 cc machines which were too rapid for the course. There was a move to have the Tourist Trophy races limited to engines of 350 cc. Fortunately reason prevailed, and as events subsequently proved, despite the additional capacity, the Senior machines have never really demonstrated that they were outstandingly quicker than 350 cc machinery —or, for that matter, in more recent times, than 250 cc and even smaller-capacity machines.

This historic 'double' led to a considerable stepping-up of AJS production, and plans were put in hand to market the ohv model. Back to the Island in 1922 came the Stevens brothers with the now classic 'big port'. On this occasion, three 350 cc Ajays were entered in the Senior, for Davies, Wade and Kelly. Only Wade finished, in 12th place. Riding in his first TT was a certain Jimmy Simpson who, although a non-finisher on a Scott, had impressed everyone during practice.

For the Junior, the riders were Sheard, Davies, Grinton, Longman, Wade, Kelly, Chambers and Harris. Once again it was an AJS triumph, the race going to Tom Sheard at 54.75 mph, with Scotsman George Grinton in second place. Chambers finished 14th.

In addition to Simpson, two other young riders who were destined to become world-famous made

1: *A historic photograph of the four Stevens brothers with the Mitchell-powered machine of 1897—the first-ever complete motorcycle built by Stevens. From left to right, George, Joe (Junior), Harry and Jack (A.J.S.).*

2: *Jack Stevens (left) and J. D. Corke on the chain-drive versions of their 1911 TT machines. Belt-drive was used in the Junior TT but, thereafter, all machines had all-chain drive. They finished in 15th and 16th places. A two-speed countershaft gearbox was employed, and front brakes were of the cycle-type stirrup pattern. Note also expansion chamber below the magneto.*

3: *The 1914 6 hp (698 cc) twin-cylinder Model D, designed for sidecar work. It had a kick-starter, fully enclosed chains and Druid forks.*

4: *Enclosed chains were also featured on the 1914 2¾ hp (349 cc) solo Model B. A two-speed or three-speed gearbox was optional.*

5: *The 1915-16 4 hp (550 cc) Model A, a 'dual-purpose' machine with non-detachable cylinder heads and sloping top-tube frame. It was a smaller-engined version of the 'D'.*

6: *A 1914 idea of the sports, or 'torpedo', aluminium sidecar attached to a 6 hp Model D. Note the elaborate chassis, anti-bounce spring on nose and windscreen security strap.*

7: *Standard 1914 Model D sidecar outfit which sold for 84 guineas. Hood, sidescreens and windshield were £3 15s extra.*

8: *Billy Jones with his fourth-place 1914 Junior TT machine which, unlike the four-speed factory entries, had three-speed transmission.*

9: *When converted to road use, although travel-stained and somewhat rusted, it was quite serviceable in the early 1950s.*

10: *Beautifully restored in 1959, the same machine as it is today. It has been regularly exhibited at the Montagu Motorcycle Museum, Beaulieu, Hants.*

11: *Enclosed chains were retained on the 1915-16 2¾ hp Model B.*

12: *Drive-side of the Model B TT Sporting. In 1916 it was listed at £55 with two-speed gear or £58 with three-speed unit.*

13: *Valve-gear side of the same model. The non-detachable cylinder heads, introduced in 1914, can be identified by the all-horizontal finning on the barrel. The machine weighed 160 lb.*

14: *The first TT victory: Cyril Williams, in the last stages of exhaustion, paddles his crippled machine towards the finish at Glencrutcherry Road. Despite pushing for nearly four miles, he was flagged almost ten minutes ahead of the second rider in this, the 1914 Junior race.*

15: *Better-known as a racing motorist and land speed record contender, Kay Don at Brooklands in 1920 with one of the earliest o v e r h e a d valve machines.*

16: *The 350 cc ohv AJS which won the Senior TT in 1921. Similar machines scored a '1-2-3' in the Junior race.*

17: *Howard Davies on a 1922 TT AJS. It was he who scored that famous Senior TT victory in 1921.*

18: *A 1920 6 hp (748 cc) Model D sidecar outfit. Later-type saddle and Terry Tan-Sad pillion were added afterwards.*

19/20: *The famous 349 cc 'Big Port' as it was in 1923, with twin pannier-type tanks and tummy-rest. For 1924, the magneto was shifted to a less vulnerable position behind the cylinder.*

21: *The 1924 349 cc Model E6, a fast-tourer which had many points of similarity with the 'Big Port'. Note alteration to frame.*

their debut in the Island. They were Stanley Woods (Cotton-Blackburne), and Wal Handley (OK-Blackburne), the latter making fastest lap in the Lightweight race.

There was no doubt whatsoever that rival manufacturers were after the AJS laurels. Bert le Vack had made a record lap in the Junior with a very special New Imperial, fitted with a three-port JAP engine designed by Val Page, the valves being operated by twin bevel, and shaft-driven overhead cams. Although a two-valve head, dual ports were used for the exhaust—a fashion that was to be reintroduced several years later. Blackburne had a range of ohv engines which had been fitted to Cotton, Rex-Acme, and the Sheffield-Henderson and took third place behind the Ajays in the Junior.

So, in 1923, AJS faced hotter opposition than they had had for years, with several new ohv machines, including a Junior Sunbeam. Jack Stevens dearly wanted to repeat that 1921 victory in the Senior, so five 'big ports' were to be ridden by Howard Davies, Syd Crabtree, C. W. Hough, J. W. Hollowell and H. F. Harris. Two finished, with Crabtree 17th and Hough 20th.

It was a ten-machine representation in the Junior, the riders being Davies, Harris, Hollowell, Hough, Sheard, Chambers, Longman, Stirling, Kelly and Simpson. The chances of a fifth successive Junior victory were decidedly good. However, it was le Vack on the ohc New Imperial who made the running, but the engine blew up and victory went to Irishman Stanley Woods on a Cotton-Blackburne, with H. F. Harris runner-up on his 'big port'. The riding of Jimmy Simpson was outstanding and he made the fastest lap at 59.59 mph. A year later, Simpson became the first rider to lap the 37¾ miles Isle of Man circuit at 60 mph, actually a staggering 64.54 mph—on a '350'! This was faster than Fred Dixon's Senior record set up later in the week on the 494 cc ohv Douglas. H. R. Scott took third place on his AJS in the Junior.

Simpson also had his eyes on the first 70 mph lap and was delighted when the Stevens brothers produced a new 498 cc ohv model. Howard Davies, hero of the 1921 races, had now emerged as a manufacturer in his own right, having designed and built the JAP-engined HRD, in both 350 cc and 500 cc form. Wal Handley (Rex-Acme-Blackburne) won the Junior, and there was a tremendous scrap between Davies and Simpson for second place. The HRD got the verdict by 40 seconds, and to Handley went fastest lap at 65.89 mph.

Jimmy Simpson retired in the Senior, but not before he had pushed the lap record up to 68.97

mph; the magic '70' was near to realisation. The race was a triumph for Howard Davies (HRD), who won at a record 66.13 mph. There was yet another exciting battle for second place, with Frank Longman (AJS) snatching the spot by just 4/5ths of a second from Alec Bennett (Norton).

That year the third sidecar race was run and AJS had the temerity to enter a 350 cc outfit against the '500s', including Norton, Douglas (with Dixon's famous banking outfit), DOT, New Hudson, P & P, P & M, Scott and Sunbeam. With George Rowley in the chair, Simpson put up a remarkable performance to finish fifth—behind Longman's 500 cc Ajay. The race went to Len Parker (Douglas), followed by the Nortons of A. E. Taylor and George Grinton. Thirty years were to pass before sidecars returned to the Island, but one feels that the Simpson/Rowley effort did a great deal to convince people that a 350 cc outfit was a perfectly practical proposition.

Jimmy himself reckons that Rowley had the worst job, keeping the light outfit on the road, more often than not with his backside scraping the 'tarmac'. The manufacturers did not exactly care for the event, especially when the daily press published many scarifying shots, which they reckoned did not do the sidecar safety image much good. Anyway, the ACU was persuaded to drop the event.

It was in 1926 that 'Jimmy the S' again made history by becoming the first rider to lap the TT course at 70 mph, taking his 500 cc AJS round at 70.43 mph. His team-mate Frank Longman took third place behind Stanley Woods (Norton) and Wal Handley (Rex-Acme). Simpson was second to Alec Bennett's Velocette in the Junior, the first victory in the Isle of Man with an overhead camshaft machine.

Since 1911, AJS had been over on the Island on ten occasions. In the Junior, the riders had scored four victories, five seconds, four thirds and three fourths. They had a first, a second, a third, and a fourth in the Senior and a fourth in the Sidecar. Seven fastest laps had also been recorded!

These were indeed the golden days of motorcycle road-racing. Inter-marque rivalry was fiercer than it had ever been. Norton, Rex-Acme, Cotton, HRD, New Imperial, New Gerrard, OK-Supreme, Velocette, Rudge, Scott, Sunbeam—these were the main rivals to AJS. It was also the era of great riders and personalities, men such as Alec Bennett, Howard Davies, Frank Longman, Jimmy Simpson, Stanley Woods, Graham Walker, Charlie Dodson, Wal Handley, Paddy Johnston, Jimmy Guthrie, the Twemlow brothers Eddie and Ken,

Bert le Vack, Syd Crabtree, H. G. Tyrell-Smith, Ernie Nott, Freddie Hicks, Fred Dixon—a wealth of talent that has never been matched since in strength of numbers.

The chain-driven overhead camshaft Ajays made their debut in the Island in 1927, and on one of them Jimmy Simpson was third in a race that was dominated by Fred Dixon on a 344 cc HRD-JAP. Jimmy reckoned that with just a little more steam he might have pipped Harold Willis (Velocette) for second place. At the end only 13 seconds separated the two riders.

AJS took push-rod machines to the Island in 1928 and George Rowley finished second behind Charlie Dodson's Sunbeam in the Senior. Once again Jimmy Simpson made fastest lap, and on a soaking wet circuit achieved a splendid 67.94 mph. He retired in both Senior and Junior, and the following year went over to Nortons. Although he never won a race for the Stevens brothers he was easily the most spectacular and popular rider of the period.

A return was made to the ohc machines for 1929, but despite his excellent second place in the previous year's Senior, George Rowley was nominated as a reserve, the team comprising Wal Handley, Tommy Spann, Frank Longman and Ronnie Parkinson. Leo Davenport was also down as a reserve. Handley shook everyone in practice on his Senior AJS with a sensational record lap in 30 minutes 50 seconds, 73.5 mph.

In the Junior, Handley was narrowly beaten by Freddie Hicks (Velocette). Rowley did get a ride in the Senior, which was a very poor race for AJS. Handley crashed on the first lap, Tommy Spann fell off on the third lap, Longman had engine trouble, and Rowley's clutch burnt out.

In 1930 AJS returned to winning form when Jimmy Guthrie won the Lightweight on the beautiful little 250 cc 'cammy' at 64.71 mph from a brace of OK-Supremes ridden by Paddy Johnston and C. S. Barrow, J. G. Lind was fifth, but Leo Davenport retired. Guthrie's was the sole success that year, George Himing and Davenport being sixth and tenth respectively in the Junior, with both Guthrie and ex-Velocette man Freddie Hicks retiring. Himing was also 12th in the Senior.

Norton, Velocette, Chater-Lea and Guzzi all had overhead camshafts but whereas they used bevel drive, AJS was alone in operating the valves by chain, with constant adjustment provided by the patented Weller chain-tensioning device. These very progressive machines were continued after the Second World War, in the shape of the 7R, or 'Boys' Racer', surely the most popular and reliable

of all clubmen's racing machines. However, there is more on both ohc types later.

Despite the Guthrie victory, nothing apparently could be done to save A. J. Stevens and Co (1914) Ltd from going into liquidation. Ownership passed to Colliers, makers of the Matchless, who, at that time, did not officially support motorcycle racing. However, the management permitted a certain amount of support to be provided for George Rowley and Freddie Hicks, whose entries had been made before the liquidation. George Himing had a private entry in the Junior, and D. Brewster in the Senior.

The Senior race was catastrophic, for poor Hicks lost his life when he crashed at Union Mills; Rowley finished ninth in the Junior, and Himing 14th. It would seem that the great days of AJS in the Isle of Man had gone!

Up until the outbreak of war, Norton, Velocette, Rudge, New Imperial, Guzzi, DKW, BMW and Excelsior were the makes that figured in the TT results sheets. AJS participation was spasmodic and unsuccessful. A seventh place in the Senior was the best AJS result—changed days certainly!

Yet the entry of the 'fours' could well have led to a turning point in AJS fortunes, and their story, plus that of the 'Porcupines', is dealt with elsewhere. Partial success did come in 1951, when Bill Doran brought his 'Porc' into second place in the Senior behind Geoff Duke's Norton. Two years later, Rod Coleman brought back the old glories by winning the Junior on the 7RC, or 'Triple Knocker', with Derek Farrant making it a 'one-two'. However, despite this resounding success, it was freely stated that the writing was on the wall where 'singles' were concerned. The 250 cc NSUs were lapping at over 90 mph and it was said that the Italians would be over in 1955 with really special road-racing equipment.

The equipment was all that, and more. Duke, Armstrong and Kavanagh on the Gilera 'fours' ran away with the Senior to finish first, second and third. Duke was reported to have achieved the very first 100 mph lap, but when the timekeepers re-checked his speed was given as 99.97 mph. How near can you get? Bob McIntyre (Norton) fought a lone battle with Bill Lomas (Guzzi) in the Junior, and finished second to the Italian twin. MV-Agusta, NSU and Guzzi triumphed in the Lightweight, and it was to be a long, long time before a British-built '250' finished in the first three in the Isle of Man.

Derek Ennett did a magnificent job by taking his 7R AJS into second place behind Ken Kavanagh's Guzzi in the 1956 Junior. In that year

Norton, AJS and Matchless followed Velocette by not fielding factory teams. British TT hopes now rested entirely on enthusiastic and clever tuners, and on the fact that racing replicas such as the 'Boys' Racer' could be purchased. A certain amount of development work was still being carried on.

TT history was now the prerogative of foreign-built machinery. In 1957 another TT milestone was reached. Bob McIntyre (Gilera) lapped at 101.12 mph, winning the Senior from John Surtees (MV-Agusta). The 'ton' was also in sight for the Juniors, for McIntyre had turned 97 mph on his Gilera.

Surtees became the next rider to put his name on the 100 mph board when he won the 1958 Senior on his MV. He improved to 101.18 mph the following year, also on an MV. By this time the ACU had realised that the specially constructed continental machines were virtually unbeatable, and also were a tremendous attraction to spectators. Some really exotic machinery was being ridden to victory by British and Commonwealth riders—machines such as the V8 Guzzi, the inclined 'four' of Gilera, with its gear-driven twin-ohc, the desmodromic-valved Ducati, and the fascinating four-cylinder MV-Agusta. AJS thinking had proved to be correct, even as far back as 1935. More's the pity that their efforts had not received the support they deserved, and that both the 'fours' of the pre-war era and the post-war 'Porcs' had to be abandoned.

Anyway the experiment of staging a production machine TT was tried in 1959, both 500 cc and 350 cc events being run in addition to the familiar 'pro' races. This was styled Formula One and proved to be a triumph for that amiable Scot, Alastair King, who pushed his 7R 'Boys' Racer' round to the tune of 94.66 mph to win the Junior and set fastest lap at 95.27 mph. Joe Potts had more than a little to do with the preparation of this machine which, with the addition of some streamlining, was ridden by his friend Bob McIntyre in the Junior TT proper (Bob had already won the Senior Formula One event on a Norton). McIntyre put on a tremendous show, pushing the MV-Agustas of Surtees and Hartle all the way, then getting between them, to the extreme discomfort of John Hartle. For four laps Bob stayed in second place; behind Hartle came the Nortons of Alastair King, Geoff Duke and Bob

Anderson. The 7R was most certainly flying.

Then the AJS ran into trouble. Excessive vibration caused the main securing brackets of the streamlined shell to crack and the structure gradually came apart. The frame lugs themselves had been damaged and he could do nothing but retire. Had it been at all possible to continue, then the Scot would have pressed on !

In 1960, McIntyre tangled with the same pair of riders again and on the same make of machine. On that occasion he finished third, and his average of 95.11 mph was the fastest ever achieved by a 350 cc 'single'. The knowledge of Jack Williams and the tuning wizardry of Joe Potts, had evolved a production 'Boys' Racer' that was only fractionally slower than the costly Italian Grand Prix machines, which money just could not buy from the factory.

The 'one-lungers' made a temporary come-back in 1961, the MVs not having too happy a time in either Senior or Junior races. Mike Hailwood (Norton) won the former, which was the first time a single-cylinder machine had averaged over 100 mph. Phil Read (Norton) lifted the Junior but, as you will read later in the chapter on the 7R, this could well have been a clear-cut victory for Mike Hailwood (7R).

The 'ton' lap still eluded the Juniors, although Gary Hocking (MV) came pretty near to it with 99.58 mph. Hailwood dearly wanted this distinction and came very close to earning it on the 7R. It would have been a splendid thing for AJS, as Jimmy Simpson had been the first to do 60 mph and then 70 mph in the 1920s.

Hailwood had his wish after all; but it was on an MV-Agusta that he set a new Junior lap record at 101.58 mph. The speeds of the 250 cc 'multis' were also becoming shattering, for Hailwood had returned 99.58 mph the previous year on his Lightweight Honda.

AJS came into the picture once more in 1964, when Phil Read and Mike Duff brought their 7Rs into second and third places in the Junior, behind Redman's winning Honda. In the 1966 Junior, Peter Williams, son of Jack, took second place in the Junior behind Agostini's MV. However, that year in the Isle of Man was to have far-reaching effects on the future of AJS, with the excellent performance of a British-built '250' in the Lightweight. This will be dealt with later in the book.

Chapter 3

the 'big port'

ALTHOUGH AMC named three models 'big ports' in the 1934 range, the first machine to carry that famed title was the 1922 Junior TT '350'. It was a development of the original 1920 ohv Ajay with which Cyril Williams won the Junior. We can trace the origins of the 'big port' to that epoch-making little machine.

When it appeared in 1920, the frame was basically that of the side-valve 1914 TT winner, and the two-gallon tank was as near-as-dammit saddle pattern. This was altered in 1921 to a more normal wedge-type, carried between the twin top-tubes. The 1920 edition did not have a separate oil-tank, but for the TT this was added, and carried on the saddle down-tube; the spring-type oil-pump was controlled from the handlebars. A sight-feed was fitted originally but dispensed with in the Isle of Man races.

The cast-iron cylinder head was held down by a flexible steel strap and had vertical finning. The valves were at an angle of 45 degrees, operated by push-rods which sloped in towards the top. The piston was also of cast-iron, having four rings. Plain bearings were used throughout, except for the single roller-bearing big-end, and a forged steel con rod was employed. The Thompson-Bennett magneto was chain-driven and mounted in a somewhat exposed position in front of the engine. An Amac carburettor was used.

The transmission of the 1920 TT winner was highly interesting, as the two-speed gearbox had additional two-speed countershaft gears producing, in all, four ratios. The arrangement was most ingenious. Two equal-sized sprockets were machined onto the clutch ring. On an extension to the crankshaft, two loosely fitted sprockets differed slightly in size. Either could be dog-engaged to the shaft sprockets by means of a handlebar control. With the smaller sprockets engaged, normal high and low ratios came into play. Engagement of the larger sprocket produced higher ratios to reduce the risk of over-running the engine on the long descent from the Mountain. Thus, in each position, there were two forward speeds.

Nevertheless, this unorthodox transmission almost cost AJS the race. On at least two of the leading machines, the dog-engagement failed and no ratios could be selected. Even the eventual winner, Williams, found the gears troublesome.

At Brooklands, on the experimental ohv machine, Howard Davies became the first rider of a '350' to achieve 80 mph. Over the flying kilometre he reached 80.67 mph and at Chepstow speed trials he recorded 81.8 mph over the flying quarter-mile. At Brooklands, he broke 12 class and eight international records.

For 1921, a normal three-speed countershaft gearbox was fitted, driven via a multi-disc, cork-insert clutch. The engine dimensions were unchanged, namely 74 × 81 mm (349 cc), but there were several detail alterations. The included angle between the valves was reduced to 40 degrees, the valves were now made of nickel-chrome, being of a hollow, trumpet-shaped pattern known better as 'tulip' valves, and the push-rods were now almost parallel.

Much stiffer steel plates were used to carry the rocker-gear and to prevent over-loading of the springs a powerful tension spring was used to interconnect the rockers. A new steel piston was fabricated with a concave head and liberally perforated with different diameter holes. The inlet and exhaust ports were of $1\frac{9}{16}$ inch diameter.

Trouble had been experienced with loss of compression on the 1920 engines, and this was traced to gas leak between head and barrel face. Both were made of cast-iron, the head being ground on to the barrel. For 1921, a patent copper-asbestos sealing gasket was employed, which was found to cure the trouble.

The TB magneto was replaced by a Lucas instrument, and foot-operation was introduced for the oil pump. More efficient Druid forks were provided, the frame generally stiffened up and, as has been mentioned, the saddle tank was replaced by a wedge-pattern located between the frame top-tubes.

This, of course, was the machine which gained the double in the TT, and the one with which Howard Davies won the Senior. 'HRD' had also been entered in the 1920 Senior with a 350 cc machine but had broken down at the start of the second lap.

Now we come to the genuine 'big port', as raced in the 1922 TT. To start with, it had interconnected front and rear internal-expanding brakes. An improved three-speed gearbox was fitted with individually ground gears, giving ratios of 8.28, 6.05 and 4.93 to 1. The saddle down tube was shortened giving a much lower riding position, and 650 × 65 mm tyres were fitted.

Different cams were used, the centre to the tip of the cam being equal to the radius of the gear wheels, and each cam was carried on ball bearings. The single-row roller big-end bearing was retained, as were the steel flywheels. The cylinder head was considerably modified and the internal diameter of the exhaust port was increased to $1\frac{5}{8}$ inch. This entailed a remarkably large-diameter exhaust pipe, which looked even larger on such a small machine. For the first time, an aluminium piston was used, still with four narrow rings. Compression ratio was 5.7 to 1. This, then, was the famed 'big port', a machine that was to launch scores of riders on successful racing careers.

At that time, the four Stevens brothers all held the leading positions in the company. Jack Stevens (AJS), MIAE, was production manager; Harry Stevens, AMIAE, was senior managing director; Joe Stevens Junior, AMIAE, was manager of the experimental section; and George Stevens acted as commercial manager.

The TT machine was exhibited in production form at the 1923 Motorcycle Show, and was styled the AJS Super Sports. It is fully described in the chapter dealing with the period 1920-1939.

The 1923 TT machines showed little change from the previous year, but the 1924 'big port' had many alterations and modifications. In fact, at first glance, it looked entirely different to any of the preceding models, and only the gold-lettered AJS on the tank was recognisable. To start with, twin $1\frac{1}{2}$-gallon petrol tanks were bolted together, gripping special lugs on the top tube. The magneto was moved from its vulnerable position in front of the engine on to a platform behind the cylinder. The engine itself looked different, mainly because of dual stays securing the more heavily finned head to the frame down-tube. The Amac carburettor was dropped in favour of the two-jet Binks 'mousetrap' screwed direct into the port.

Dry-sump lubrication was adopted, circulated from a 'Rotoplunge' pressure and scavenge pump. The angle between the valves was increased to 42 degrees but a revolutionary feature was that the inlet valve had a much larger diameter than the exhaust. The 'big port' was reduced slightly to $1\frac{1}{2}$ inch diameter, and the inlet was $1\frac{11}{16}$ inch. The valve lift from the steep-sided cams was $\frac{5}{16}$ inch, with an overlap of 40 degrees. Dual concentric valve springs were employed. The tappets, operating light push-rods, bore directly on to the cams without followers. The overhead rocker arms were splined to the bearing tubes which were impregnated with graphite. Compression ratio was raised to 6 to 1, entailing the use of a flat-top aluminium piston with cut-away sections to avoid the valves. Again, a three-speed gearbox was used in conjunction with multi-plate cork clutch; ratios were 9.91, 6.47 and 5.27 to 1.

This model was the mainstay of the AJS racing effort, resulting in countless successes all over the world. It was made also in 498 cc form from 1926 and was the first machine to attain a 70 mph lap in the TT. The ohc machines were used for the 1927 TT, but in 1928 AJS reverted to the 'big ports', which was the last time they were used for racing by the factory.

Sand-racing, grass-track, sprints, speed hill-climbs, trials, scrambles, circuit events—wherever there was motorcycle sport the 'big port' was to be found. Long before special speedway machines were evolved, when dirt-track racing was popularised in Australia, the 'big port' Ajays provided the mainstay of the new sport. The factory did consider building a speedway machine but, after many discussions, decided that it was not a practical proposition in view of their racing and production commitments.

During the 1920s, sand-racing was extremely popular, with big meetings at places like Southport, Saltburn, Pendine, St Andrews and Kirkcaldy. Jimmy Simpson was a formidable competitor on a 'big port'. However, the 'King of the Sands' was undoubtedly Ronnie Parkinson, another 'big port' exponent who, when his machines were functioning, was practically invincible in the 350 cc classes and was invariably up with the big stuff in unlimited events.

Sprints were also the happy hunting-grounds of the 'big ports' and here again, Simpson, Parkinson and Rowley were prominent. The lightweight AJS, with its high power-output from a highly tuned engine, was ideal.

There were few opportunities for road-racing on the mainland in these days, apart from the small circuit at Syston Park. Brooklands did not attract some riders because the technique for track-racing was somewhat specialised. True, there were the Amateur Road-Races in September in the Isle of Man but these, like racing in Ireland and abroad, were not always within the pocket of the average club rider. This accounted for the scores of grass-track meetings held up and down the country where, again, the 'big port' AJS was eminently successful.

Chapter 4

the 'cammy' AJS

TOWARDS THE END of 1926, AJS felt that the 'big port', fast as it undoubtedly was, would become rapidly outclassed when some of the latest engines were fully developed. Secrets were hard to keep in the motorcycle industry and it was known that Walter Moore (later of NSU fame) was working on a new overhead camshaft unit for Norton. The Velocette was already regarded as a formidable contender, Alec Bennett having defeated Jimmy Simpson's push-rod AJS in the 1926 Junior and, to Simpson's disgust, making the fastest lap with the new ohc machine—the first-ever set in the Island by a 'cammy' machine. Chater-Lea also had an ohc engine, designed by Doug Marchant. On this '350' he had achieved a lap at over 100 mph at Brooklands.

So, Chief Engineer Phil Walker was entrusted with the design of an engine that, in the years to come, was to provide AJS with one of the most successful competition machines ever evolved— an engine that was to be widely imitated, especially by continental manufacturers.

Walker located the camshaft across the cylinder head, driven by a long chain automatically kept in correct tension by the ingenious Weller device, which had been used by A. C. Bertelli on the single-ohc, chain-driven Aston Martin car engine. It had also been used with outstanding success on aero engines. The drive was enclosed in an aluminium casing, on the outside of which was mounted the oil pump. Dry-sump lubrication was fitted, and AJS had now gone over to caged-roller big-end bearings. The head had deep, vertical fins, and the magneto was somewhat vulnerably placed in front of the frame down-tube. The new engine was actually installed in the 'big-port' frame.

Jimmy Simpson took third place in the 1927 Junior with the new 'cammy', and then went abroad to win the 350 cc races in the Swiss, Belgian and European Grands Prix. AJS felt that they had a worthy successor to the 'big port' and replicas were listed for 1929. It was in this year that the name Amal appeared for the first time, followed by the amalgamation of three famous carburettor firms, Binks, Amac and B and B (Brown and Barlow).

Curiously enough, AJS went back to push-rod engines for the 1928 TT, with the addition of new leading-link front forks. George Rowley took

second place in the Senior and Simpson, as usual, made fastest lap. Best placing in the Junior was sixth, another machine being retired.

For 1929, the ohc engine was reinstated in a new frame and with the now-fashionable saddle-tank. Bigger brakes were fitted, lubrication re-designed and petrol tankage increased. It was also produced in 500 cc form and, to the dismay of Ajay fans, the tanks had either maroon or purple centre-panels. Although Wal Handley took second place in the Junior, the 'cammy' Ajays fell victims to several mechanical disorders in the Senior. Handley retired following a crash, and Spann, Rowley and Longman all abandoned. It was obvious that something would have to be done to improve the 'cammy' Ajays.

Freddie Hicks (Velocette) had beaten Wal Handley (AJS) by a whisker in the 1929 Junior

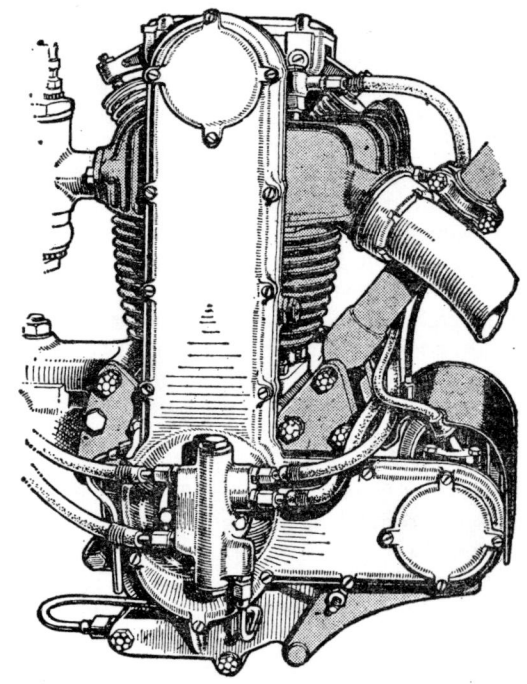

The 498 cc version of the 1929 TT overhead camshaft engine. The chain-drive was also featured on the post-war 7R 'Boys' Racer' unit, introduced in 1947, many examples of which are still being raced successfully in 1969—seven years after production ceased. 'Motor Cycling'.

TT. As a result, Hicks accepted an offer to join A. J. Stevens and Co Ltd to develop the 1930 ohc models for the TT.

The 1929 bore and stroke engine was retained and indeed, this remained unchanged until the Second World War intervened. The bigger brakes, frame-stiffening stay and cam-box scavenger pump were also incorporated in the 1930 machines. Also, Ajay fans were glad to see the dropping of the maroon-panelled petrol tank in favour of the classic black and gold finish.

Hicks devised a new and more massive frame with a single top-tube, and the girder forks now included idler bearings for the spindles. Again, the large centre-spring was retained. In addition to the 350 cc and 500 cc models, a '250' was built, to be ridden by Jimmy Guthrie. As already described in the TT chapter, the 'wee cammy' won, and the odds are that, had the concern not been taken over in 1931 by Colliers, a replica would have gone into production. A second machine was built, and finished fifth.

After the victory, the 250 cc machines were never raced by the factory again. However, one of them achieved many successes in south of England grass-track meetings. Hicks raced in the 1930 Junior, but retired.

When the 1931 TT loomed, the old company was in the process of the take-over. Freddie Hicks and George Rowley both appeared with Junior and Senior machines with a certain amount of factory backing. It was altogether a disastrous outing. Freddie Hicks lost his life (he crashed at Union Mills when in fourth place, chasing the Nortons) and Rowley finished ninth in the Junior.

The Wolverhampton factory was closed down and AJS moved to the home of their new masters, H. Collier and Sons Ltd, at Plumstead, near Woolwich—surely the most unsuitable site for a motorcycle factory it would be possible to find. Located just off one of the busiest roads in the London area, deliveries by road from the Midlands components makers were usually delayed. With AJS and Matchless now under one roof, difficulties began to become even greater.

For two years the 'cammy' machines remained dormant. Racing had been outlawed by the Colliers. George Rowley had joined the firm and converted one of the 1930 TT machines into a trials bike. In the 1932 International Six Days George was a member of the winning British International Trophy team.

Rowley fell foul of the management when one of the original 1930 TT machines was freighted back to the UK from Italy, some six months later

than it ought to have been. The delay was not the fault of the freight company, and they asked for £10 for transport charges, which the motorcycle concern refused to pay. Colliers did not want to know. The 350 cc machine could stay where it was for all they cared.

The story goes that George Rowley sneaked down to Dover, paid over a tenner, and took the machine back to the factory, where he hid it under a tarpaulin. It seemed to be in splendid nick, so without telling the bosses he quietly entered the Ajay in the 350 cc and 500 cc classes of the Brooklands 100 Miles Grand Prix.

When the entry lists were published by Bemsee, journalists seized on the presence of an AJS with works-rider George Rowley in the saddle as a pointer to a return to racing by the factory. Harry Collier was livid, but somehow saw the humour of the situation and Rowley was allowed to keep his entries.

George did fairly well in both races and would have finished much higher than fifth in the Junior had not a natural rubber petrol pipe disintegrated to cause a complete fuel blockage. He took seventh spot in the Senior in the company of most of Europe's latest and fastest '500s'.

Harry Collier sent for Rowley the following Monday. George fully expected to be fired but the Chairman congratulated him on his performance on the Saturday, and came up with the unexpected news that the directors had decided to re-enter racing and to continue development on the ohc engine. So, for 1933, a racing edition was marketed, and there was also a Trophy trials model to cash in on the ISDT success of 1932.

Harry Collier also mentioned that the future policy would be to build sufficient racing and competition models to pay for such activities. As a result, the 'cammy' Ajay emerged in what was really an entirely new form. There were several engine modifications, including the magneto which was moved from its vulnerable spot in front of the crankcase to a platform behind the cylinder. A different frame was devised, and the close-ratio four-speed gearbox was supplied with a positive foot-change. Lubrication was drastically altered, the scavenge pump now being mounted above the camshaft chain cover and driven from the offside of the camshaft.

The racing machine was supplied with a straight-through exhaust pipe, and Brooklands 'can' if required, rearward footrests and a tuned engine with the choice of three pistons giving compression ratios of 7.5, 9.0, or 11.0 to 1. The Trophy model had the low-compression piston, upswept exhaust pipe with tubular silencer and steel crankcase guard. Both models were offered at the most attractive prices of £65 for the '350', and £70 for the '500'.

Grays, the big motorcycle dealers, secured a batch of 350 cc 'cammies', probably built up from components in stock, brought from Wolverhampton, and now obsolete in so far as Colliers were concerned. It is likely that the Plumstead people allocated a selection of the later frames, wheels, mudguards and so on to complete the deal. Offered at £48, the Grays' Ajays sold like hot-cakes. Rowley and his men had adapted the engines to incorporate the latest type of scavenge pump, but owners found that drive-shaft breakages were frequent, and invariably oil was splattered all over machine and rider. They were also inclined to introduce valves more closely to pistons. Nevertheless, when these troubles had been sorted out, the bargain basement 'cammies' proved to be very competitive.

It was too late to have official entries in the 1933 TT, but the usual AJS participation was maintained with a singleton private entry in the Junior, which failed to finish. For 1934, near-standard production machines appeared, taking an 11th place in the Junior (Rowley), and 7th, 9th, and 12th in the Senior.

The Trophy model had been quietly dropped, production being concentrated on the racing machine. The 1934 engines were different in that horizontal cylinder head finning was adopted, and on the TT machines hairpin valve springs were used for the first time; long, external holding-down bolts securing the bi-metal cylinder head.

These 1934 machines were considered to be far too heavy, and for 1935 a considerable amount of electron and light-alloy material was employed, bringing the total weight of the '350' to the satisfactory figure of 260 lb. Despite the intention to produce replicas of the controversial 'fours' none was ever built for sale. Meanwhile steady development work continued on the ohc models. Everything that had proved to be satisfactory in racing was incorporated in the following year's models. The oil pumps were modified, Burman gearboxes adopted, the front forks had additional check springs, the magneto was re-located on a sloping platform, and larger petrol tanks fitted.

In 1937, the racing policy was advanced a stage further when Colliers announced that, after the TT, absolute replicas would be marketed at a price of £87 5s. These would have the new double-loop frame with single down-tube, megaphone exhaust systems would be incorporated, and each machine would be individually tested at Brooklands.

In 1938, a new spring frame was employed on the TT machines which comprised short pivoted arms to which were attached spring boxes located top and bottom within the main frame-tubes. This machine was in reality the forerunner of the 'Boys' Racer', dealt with in the next chapter.

Chapter 5

7R the 'boys' racer'

KNOWN AFFECTIONATELY as the 'Boys' Racer', the 7R AJS was surely the most successful production racing machine of all time. Based on the pre-war 'cammy' Ajay, it remained in production from 1949 till 1962, and its first appearance was in the 1948 Pau Grand Prix with Fergus Anderson in the saddle. He had worked himself up to second place but had to retire with a burnt-out clutch. Much of the pre-production testing had been done by Jock West.

Word of the 7R quickly got about. At a price of £316 4s 8d, including purchase tax, it was easily the bargain of the year to the race-minded man. It was a good looker and, as supplied to the customer, was fitted with a truly enormous megaphone exhaust. Ready for racing it weighed around 285 lb.

The chain-driven, overhead camshaft engine developed 30 bhp at 7,000 rpm which, with a top gear ratio of 5.14 to 1, gave a theoretical top speed of 106 mph—not at all bad for a '350'! Among the early purchasers were Maurice Cann, Syd Barrett, Les Dear, and Eric MacPherson. Ernie Lyons rode a Tom Arter-entered model to victory in the 1948 Leinster '200' (350 cc category). By the time the TT came round in June, AJS had the huge representation of 25 machines in the Junior with Ted Frend, Jock West and Les Graham on factory-entered models which differed little from the production versions.

Yet, the machines were not quite quick enough to cope with the Nortons and the Velocettes, the best position being Maurice Cann's fifth place on his privately-entered machine. However, the reliability of the 7R 'Boys' Racer' was most impressive, for of the 25 7R starters, 18 finished, in the order of 5, 8, 11, 12, 13, 14, 15, 16, etc.

One of the complaints made by riders was that the rear suspension rapidly became 'tired' on the Isle of Man circuit due to the dampers losing their effectiveness. Also, like other machines of the period, the megaphone exhaust system left little or nothing in the way of useable power 'downstairs', the urge not coming in till at least 'five-five'. Consequently full use had to be made of the gearbox, and the majority of riders discovered that much lower gear ratios were necessary. This, of course, was something that could be put right.

AJS on the whole were more than satisfied with the showing of the 'Boys' Racer'. Matt Wright, who knew more about the 'cammy' engine than anyone else, re-joined the company and immediately set about improving the torque characteristics. He altered the combustion space shape to give a flatter head and played about with valve angles, finally reducing them from 80 to 74 degrees. This remained unchanged throughout the life of the 7R. Wright also opted for a much stiffer flywheel and big-end assembly. Oil drag had been suspected on the 1948 engines, so the flywheels were reduced in diameter to eliminate 'pick-up'. He also carried out several mods to the dry-sump lubrication system, and adopted separate lubrication for the primary drive. Compression ratio was upped to 8.85 to 1, the inlet valve diameter increased, and when the engine was put on the Heenan and Froude dynamometer it showed 32 bhp at 7,200 rpm. The torque was also improved, power now coming in at 5,000 rpm. Wright had experimented wtih many different types of exhaust, finally deciding on one with a much smaller megaphone.

In the 1949 Junior TT, Les Graham and Bill Doran were eliminated with gearbox failure, so the transmission was revised with different bearings, the clutch strengthened, and alterations made to the foot-change mechanism. The remarkable number of 41 'Boys' Racers' had started, and 32 had finished—another splendid demonstration of reliability, with the order 5, 8, 11, 12, 13, 14, etc.

The suspension 'jam-pots' were enlarged, and the front forks modified with a light-alloy top-lug replacing the steel one formerly employed. The one-gallon oil tank was made slimmer, riders having complained that the original fatter pattern formed a sort of built-in central heating system, which led to partially-scorched legs.

In the 1950 Junior the machines were much faster, but still not quick enough to beat the Nortons, for which make Artie Bell, Geoff Duke and Harold Daniell scored a 'one-two-three', Les Graham and Ted Frend coming in fourth and fifth respectively on their 'Boys' Racers'. Abroad, the 7R was becoming more and more prominent, many successes being secured by such riders as the Monnerets, *père et fils*, Reg Armstrong, Erge, and Bill Petch. For the 'Continental Circus' a 7R was an excellent investment, and rarely have machines been raced regularly without experiencing major

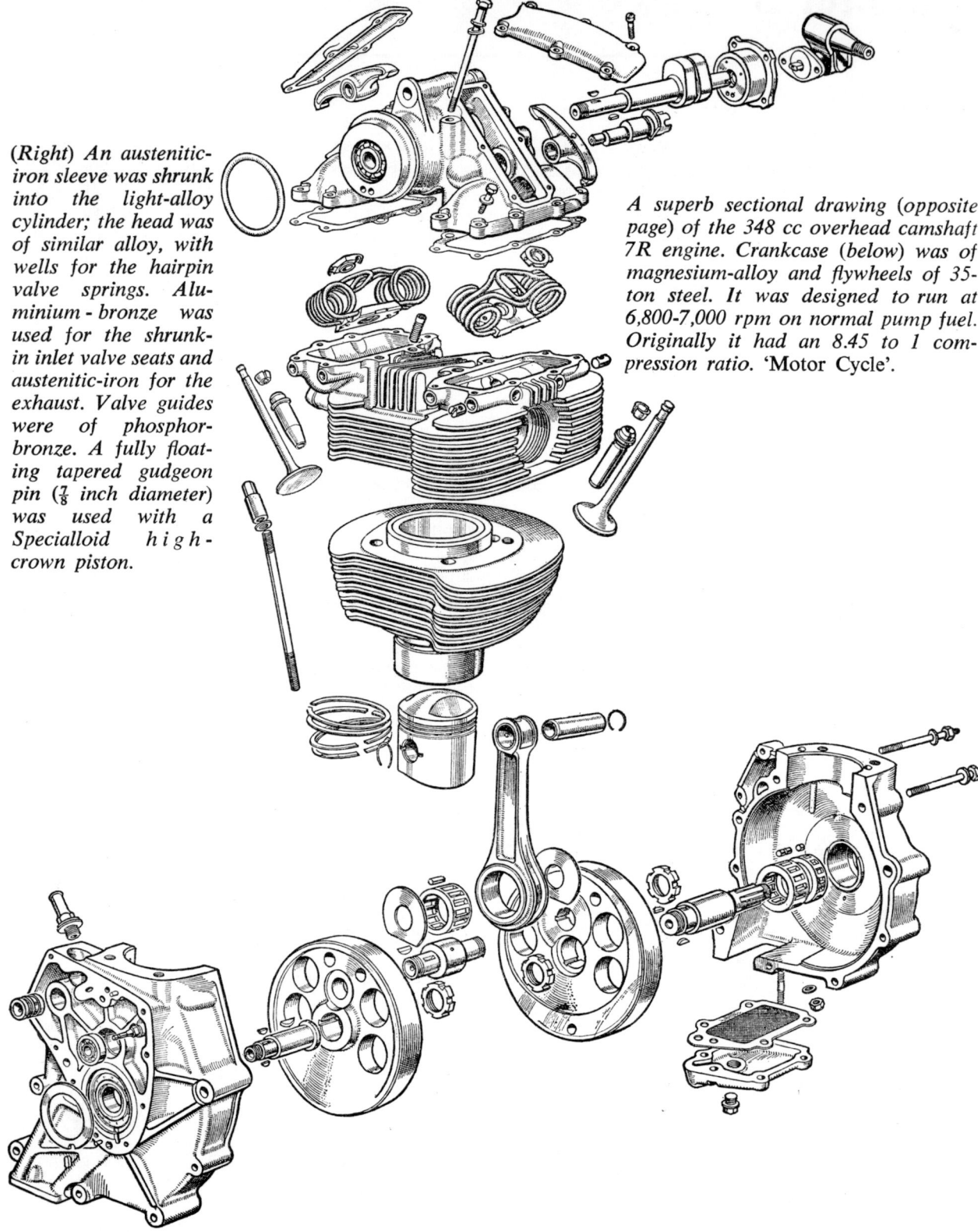

(*Right*) *An austenitic-iron sleeve was shrunk into the light-alloy cylinder; the head was of similar alloy, with wells for the hairpin valve springs. Aluminium - bronze was used for the shrunk-in inlet valve seats and austenitic-iron for the exhaust. Valve guides were of phosphor-bronze. A fully floating tapered gudgeon pin ($\frac{7}{8}$ inch diameter) was used with a Specialloid h i g h - crown piston.*

A superb sectional drawing (opposite page) of the 348 cc overhead camshaft 7R engine. Crankcase (below) was of magnesium-alloy and flywheels of 35-ton steel. It was designed to run at 6,800-7,000 rpm on normal pump fuel. Originally it had an 8.45 to 1 compression ratio. 'Motor Cycle'.

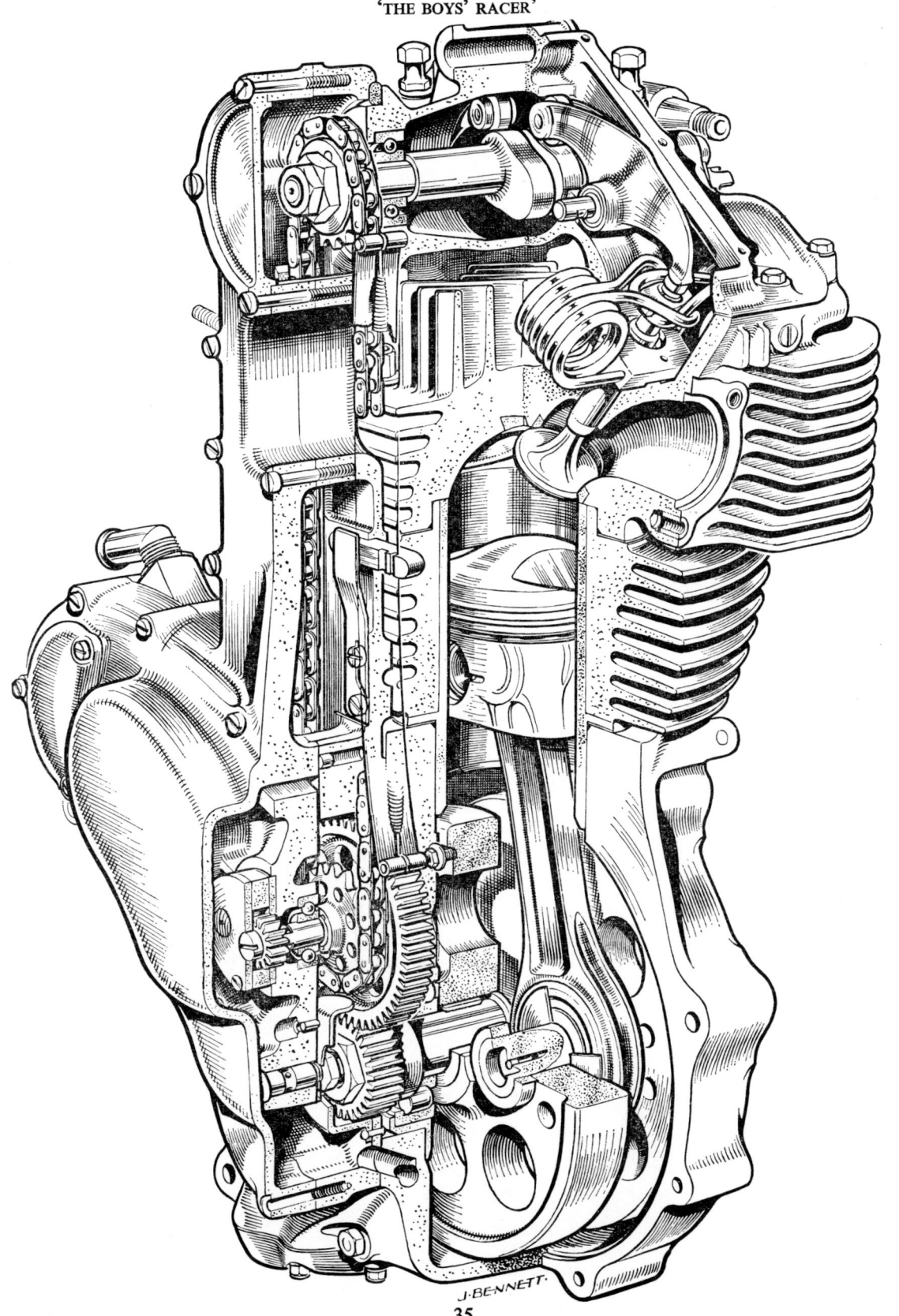

J·BENNETT·

mechanical disasters and complete rebuilds.

Yet some riders criticised the handling. The big 'jam pots' still did not appear to provide the answer to the loss of suspension effectiveness. Matt Wright attempted in vain to get the management interested in replacing the AJS system with Girling proprietary units. It was to be some while before this was done, and it wasn't in Matt Wright's time.

For 1951, the 7R had something of a face-lift, mainly due to the adoption of 19 inch wheels, re-designed Teledraulic forks, and clip-on handle-bars. Compression ratio went up to 9.4 to 1, and different cams were employed with a more efficient method of lubricating them. Power output had been stepped up to 34 bhp at 7,200 rpm.

Les Graham had left AJS to ride for MV-Agusta, and the works trio for the 1951 Junior now comprised Reg Armstrong, Bill Doran and Mike Featherstone. As in 1950, the Nortons were just that bit faster, although Doran chased Duke, Lockett and Brett for four laps, until engine trouble intervened. Armstrong and Featherstone then assumed fourth and fifth places and seemed likely to finish in that order, when Reg had his primary chain break, two miles from the finish. He pushed to the finish but by the time he reached the chequered flag he had dropped to 23rd place, with Featherstone fourth. Armstrong was dubbed a member of the 'Pushers' Club', along with former Ajay riders Les Graham and Cyril Williams. As you will see in the chapter dealing with the Manx Grand Prix, the story was altogether different, the 'Boys' Racer' proving more than a match for their rivals.

For 1953, the 7R was re-vamped, taking on quite a different appearance. For one thing a completely new frame was devised, with a narrow cradle carrying the power-unit. The older steel plates were scrapped in favour of an aluminium bridge-piece, which also served as an anchorage for the top of the gearbox. The bottom engine and gearbox fixing pivots bolts were secured via flanged bushes welded into holes drilled in the frame tubes. This produced a much more rigid assembly than on previous models.

Modifications to the engine included stiffening the bottom-end, altering the valve rockers to roller-

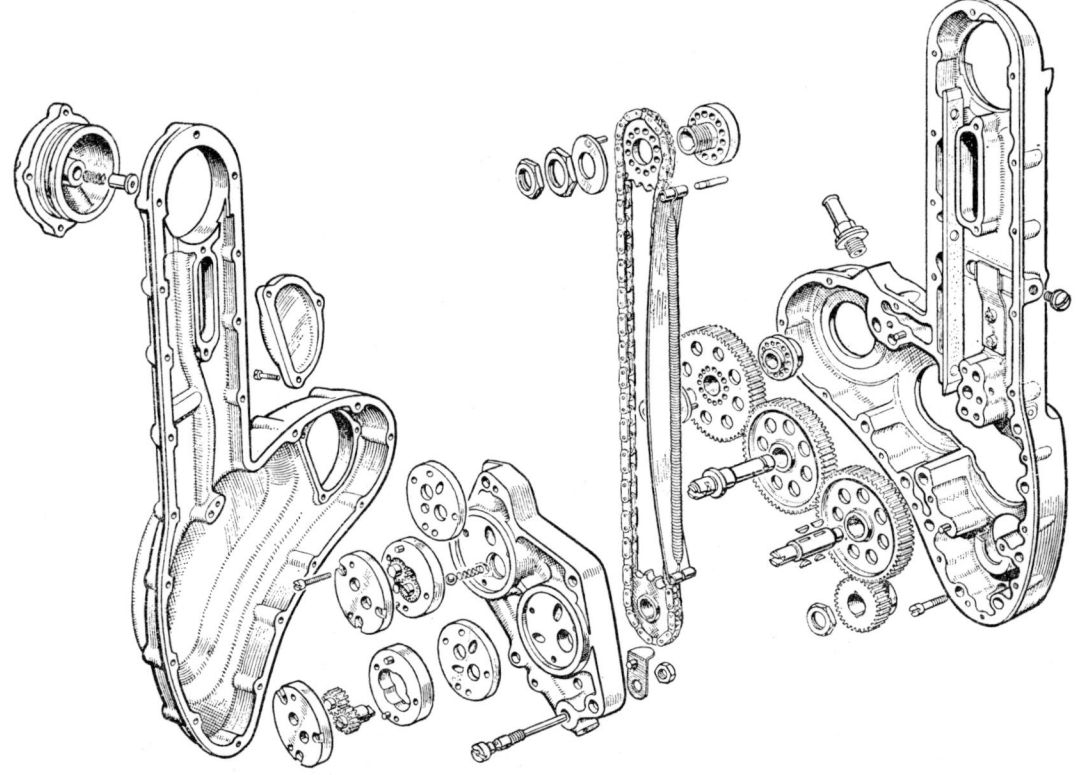

Details of the chain-drive to the overhead camshafts on the 7R engine, showing the Weller tensioning device, also used on pre-war 'cammy' units. Twin oil pumps were driven by the timing-pinion spindles. Magneto was driven via spur gears and the chain.

type cams, and reducing the width of the crankpin, to produce a more compact crankcase. The familiar stiffening ribs were dispensed with altogether. The old screw-type exhaust fitting gave way to a flange, secured by three Allen screws. This was not too popular with mechanics, should urgent repairs have to be effected. Whenever one heard a bellow of pain, followed by a stream of curses, one knew instinctively that someone was trying to remove the exhaust pipe from a hot engine !

A 5½-gallon petrol tank was fitted, secured by a spring-loaded metal strap. The tank itself was located to the frame by rubber bushes and pegs, the front ones being fully adjustable to allow for the fitting of smaller and even 'sprint' tanks. The 19 inch wheels were retained, but the front carried a narrower (2.75 × 19 inch) ribbed tyre, with 3.25 × 19 inch at the rear. The saddle was the fashionable short pattern with raised rear portion. Around this time a great deal of thought had been going into seating, and those of the period now look strange compared with the modern 'chaise-longue' types.

An AJS won the 1954 Junior, with Rod Coleman up. However, this was achieved on the 'Triple Knocker', with which I will deal at the end of this chapter. Jack Williams came to AMC as Chief Development Engineer in 1954. He had done a considerable amount of work on the three-valve engine, before the company decided that it was not an economical proposition, and he then went to work on the 7R.

C. J. Williams, AMMechE, has always been a brilliant engineer and approaches every problem from a scientific angle. He had ridden in the TT from 1929 to 1938, mainly on Raleigh and Vincent-HRD and had done a major portion of the development work on these makes. He did not use rule of thumb methods, but the application of sound engineering principles before putting anything into practice. When he inherited the 7R, the engine was producing 37 bhp at 7,500 rpm, but when production ceased in 1962 Jack Williams had stepped this up to 42 bhp at 7,800 rpm, with great reliability into the bargain. So let us see how he set about doing this.

Williams first of all concentrated on improving the breathing of the engine, and obtaining the best possible bmep figures. He never was a believer in revs for revs' sake, disliking anything which would tend to over-tax the valve gear without producing anything tangible in the way of power output. In the case of the 7R engine, he began to experiment with ports and, to study the effect of air-flow and

so forth, he evolved a special Williams test-rig.

Vic Willoughby of *The Motor Cycle* once gave a most accurate description of the various methods used by Williams in overcoming the lack of proper test equipment by making his own apparatus. For air-flow experiments he constructed a dummy cylinder, which had a detachable wooden head, to which could be fitted different ports. The shape of these could be altered speedily by the use of Harbutt's Plasticine. Air was drawn through the port and the cylinder by means of a pump, being controlled by a normal inlet valve. Varying sizes and shapes of valves could be tried and the amount of lift altered at will.

To study the effect of passing mixture through the head, he lined the inside of the cylinder with white cardboard. Accurately measured amounts of petrol were mixed with coloured dyes before being injected into the air-stream. Thus he could see virtually at a glance where the petrol droplets were going when inside the cylinder head. A later modification was the adoption of a Monometer, by which the air-flow coefficient could be calculated accurately.

After many experiments, Williams came to the conclusion that a down-swept port shape was superior to a flat port, although the actual breathing properties were not quite so good. However, it produced a much-improved mixture distribution, and following further experiments when the port was straightened out from the entrance to the valve, a definite increase of up to three bhp was the resultant dividend. Also, volumetric efficiency had been improved to the extent that all-round fuel consumption was reduced to a marked degree. It was also found possible to bring the amount of ignition advance forward from 39 degrees to 37 degrees BTDC.

Jack also experimented with the 'squish' pattern piston and head, improving both bottom and top end performance with a 'squish-gap' of 25-30 thou. The anti-detonating properties of the new piston, head and altered porting, enabled the compression ratio to be lifted from the old ceiling of 10.8 to 1 to 12.2 to 1.

There were other modifications to be taken into consideration, notably in relation to carburation, inlet tract length and valve seat shape. He finally settled on a 1¾ inch carburettor choke and the inlet tract from bellmouth to valve head was increased to 13¼ inch. The 1956 engine had the bore and stroke altered to the 'near-square' dimensions of 75.5 × 78 mm. Safe rpm limit had gone up to 'seven-eight'.

Yet even before the 75.5 × 78 mm engine was

available the Jack Williams mods were already paying dividends, particularly in short-circuit races on the Continent and in the Manx Grand Prix races. Although the Nortons still had a slight edge on the 'Boys' Racers' when factory teams met, there was very little in it.

In the 1955 Junior, the AMC entries were virtually 'off the peg' machines with no additional streamlining. Sole concession to aerodynamics was a re-shaped petrol tank so that the riders' knees could be tucked in out of the air-stream. The following year, Derek Ennett was second in the Junior and the team of 'Boys' Racers' took the manufacturer's team prize.

The reliability of the 7Rs became a by-word, and after AMC opted out of racing, the tuners took over. People like Tom Arter and Bill Bancroft came on the scene, the latter entering a 7R prepared by Joe Potts of Bellshill, Scotland, with which Alan Shepherd won the 1958 Manx Grand Prix. It was Potts and his friend Alastair King who gave Bob McIntyre his chance in big-time racing. Bob made all the Norton and Velocette boys go home from Silverstone with their tails between their legs by winning that year's Bemsee Hutchinson '100' at the then prodigious speed of 92.88 mph. When McIntyre shook Surtees and Hartle on their MV-Agustas in the 1959 Junior TT it was excessive vibration that led to the retirement of his 7R. Other riders also complained of this, and it was a problem which Jack Williams had to solve.

At Plumstead there was always a marked objection to any technician seeking assistance from outside the factory. Thus, when Williams asked for an electronic installation to attempt to trace the source of the vibration, his request was turned down. He was also refused permission to borrow a Lucas rig. Therefore he counted it a major victory when he managed to persuade Mr D. S. Heather and the directors to change the suspension to Girling, as Matt Wright had tried in vain to do several years earlier.

Being Williams, he was determined to discover the cause of the vibration and, with testers John Clarke and Frank Perris, set about the task wholeheartedly. He first checked carefully that there was no sign of undue vibration, right throughout the rpm range, when the engine was run on the bench. Yet, back in the frame, the vibration was most pronounced. Eventually it was traced to the aluminium bridge-piece; sympathetic vibrations were being transmitted to the frame via the gearbox mountings. By modifying the engine-cum-gearbox mounting piece, so that the box was held by steel plates to the engine and not directly to the

frame, the trouble vanished completely. Earlier 7Rs also had a bad habit of shedding their carburettors, but during Williams' time this had been cured by using flexible mountings.

The 'Boys' Racers' continued to earn their keep, and I believe that it will be interesting to give the full specification of the 1960 7R.

Engine: Chain-driven, overhead camshaft. 75.5 × 78 mm, 349 cc, 11.6 to 1 compression ratio. 42 bhp at 7,800 rpm. Valve timing, inlet opens 55 deg BTDC, closes 78 deg ATDC. Exhaust opens, 78 deg BTDC, closes 44 deg ATDC. Ignition (magneto), 33.5 deg. Light-alloy cylinder head; shrunk-in valve seats; sodium-cooled exhaust valves; duplex overlapping hairpin valve springs; roller cam followers; eccentric rocker spindle. Weller chain-tensioner with friction damper; Grand Prix Amal (T5GP) carburettor, with 1⅜ in choke and 330 jet; magnesium crankcase, cam box and timing case; KE 805 forged steel con rods; two-piece crankpin; caged roller-bearing big-end; light-alloy cylinder muff with iron liners; dry-sump lubrication with large-size feed and scavenge pumps.

Transmission: Four-speed AMC gearbox with positive-stop foot-change; pivot mounting and draw-bolt adjustment. Ratios 8.68, 6.46, 5.36 and 4.87 to 1. Sprocket sizes: engine 23 teeth, clutch 42, gearbox 21, rear wheel 56. Exposed multi-plate clutch with Ferodo inserts.

Frame: Duplex cradle, one-piece swinging-arm rear suspension of welded construction; conical magnesium hub-castings. 8 inch diameter light-alloy brake drums with shrunk-in iron hubs. Straight-spoked wheels with light-alloy rims. 2.75 × 19 in Dunlop tyres (front), 3.25 × 19 in (rear).

General: 5-gallon petrol tank; 7-pint oil tank. Tachometer flexibly mounted in glass fibre front number carrier. Rear racing number plates. Glass fibre racing seat with back-rest. 'Perspex' handlebar-type screen; clip-on racing handlebars, with steering damper. AJS Teledraulic forks. Spring-up racing filler caps. Adjustable chain-oiler. Racing ball-ended controls. Speed-action twist-grips.

Dimensions, etc: Overall length, 6 ft 8 in. Height, 3 ft 1 in. Width, 2 ft 0 in. Wheelbase, 4 ft 7 in. Seat height, 2 ft 7 in. Ground clearance, 6.75 in. Weight, 285 lb.

These machines were very much hand-made in the racing department, and naturally every single component was carefully balanced. Great attention was paid to the finish, and nuts and bolts were either castellated or wired on.

Alan Shepherd made the headlines in the 1960 Ulster Grand Prix when he stayed with John Surtees on the leading MV-Agusta until eliminated by that rarest of happenings, a broken camshaft chain. AJS have always maintained that this was the sole occasion when a 7R was put out of a race by any form of chain breakage in the ohc drive. The speed of Shepherd's 'Boys' Racer' matched that of the Italian 'four' and so rapid was the 7R that after the race the MV-Agusta team-manager put in an official protest to the organisers, implying that the engine was over-size. It was stripped down, miked, and found to be exactly 349.08 cc !

World Champion John Surtees in his book *Speed* (published by Arthur Barker) comments: 'I was the only MV-Agusta rider in the race and, as it so turned out, I found some remarkably tough opposition from rather an unexpected quarter, a privately entered AJS, ridden by Alan Shepherd. For six laps he kept up a very close chase, never more than a few yards behind me . . .'

Incidentally, although Surtees was a great admirer of the 7R, he never actually rode one in a race. He did construct the frame of the Arter-AJS which Mike Duff later rode with such verve, fitting a 7R engine into a very much-modified Norton 'Featherbed' frame. John was invited to ride a 'Porcupine' in the 1953 Ulster Grand Prix but had to decline owing to an arm injury not having healed up properly. Anyway John told me not so long ago that, when he originally built the Arter-AJS, it was some 40 lb lighter than the production 7R. He fully intended to race it himself but, as he was in the process of purchasing a business, the machine went in order to swell his capital.

Jack Williams continued with his development programme, designing a new cam and changing the valve spring material to Swedish steel. It is alleged that, before coming up with the answer in relation to the new cam, it took Jack over 100 hours, and hundreds of sheets of foolscap, before the required shape was found. Later he managed to check his calculations on a computer, and the entire operation took him exactly ten minutes !

The tremendous improvements to the 7R were never more apparent than when Mike Hailwood rode a privately-entered one in the 1961 Junior; he was literally robbed of victory just 15 miles from the finish, when a gudgeon pin let go ! Mike had been lapping at 96-97 mph, only fractionally slower than the Italian 'fours', and quicker than any 350 cc 'single' had ever gone before. Mike's father, Stan Hailwood, purchased a 7R which had run in that 1961 race, and on it 'Mike the Bike' won the 350 cc event at Oliver's Mount, Scarborough, at record speed and with a new lap record.

In the Manx races in September the 7Rs took the first three places in the Junior. It was wet during the race, but on the two-mile straight past the Highlander both Neville and Reynolds had been timed exceeding 115 mph—neither of them having any form of streamlining whatsoever.

By this time AMC were feeling the pinch financially, and there could be no question of going racing. Even the construction of 7Rs came under the hammer, for they were now regarded as being prestige exercises and each individual machine was reportedly built at a loss. Anyway, the decision was made to cease production in 1962, although a handful were completed in the early part of 1963.

Jack Williams was able to transmit a great deal of his eight years of living with the 7R to the tuning folk, who obtained wonderfully successful results for many years after the 'Boys' Racer' had disappeared from the AMC lists. Tom Arter, Tom Kirby, Joe Potts and others continued development work on their own.

There have been many suggestions for improving the basic 7R power-unit. I do know that plans were in hand for the production of a replacement barrel, piston and con rod to give a bore and stroke of 81×68 mm, but I never heard of anyone actually constructing these bits and pieces.

When the Vanwall racing car engine was revealed in 1957 as having titanium con rods, the late Tony Vandervell pointed out to me that Jack Williams had used this material from time to time for rockers and rods since 1955. Vandervell was always motorcycle engine-minded, and quite openly admitted that in the construction of their World Championship-winning $2\frac{1}{2}$-litre engine a good deal of expertise was 'borrowed' from AJS and Norton.

The Junior TT victory by Rod Coleman in 1954 was on the 'Triple Knocker' or, to give it its factory designation, the 7R3. It was the work of Ike Hatch, who had been responsible for that complex design the four-valve ohc Excelsior, with which Syd Gleave won the 1933 Lightweight. Hatch had inherited the original racing 'cammy' AJS engine in the 1930s from Phil Walker, and had now returned to the company as Chief Development Engineer following the take-over of A. J. Stevens and Co Ltd by the Colliers.

One could scarcely state that the 'Triple Knocker' was an attractive engine; in fact it definitely looked unbalanced owing to the disposition of the timing case for the overhead camshaft chain-drive. Based on the 7R, the case sloped backwards, to permit the drive to be taken direct to the inlet camshaft, which was placed transversely across the inlet valve. Where the cam-box had formerly been located a parallel lay-shaft was driven by spur gears; this shaft drove two separate camshafts via bevel gears and these, in turn, operated the two radial exhaust valves. The sparking plug was placed between the two exhaust camshafts, and the bottom half of the engine was basically 7R.

Chief argument against the 7R3 was that, despite the elaborate method of operating the valves by chain, shafts and bevels, the power-output was little different from that of the TT version of the 7R. Also, riders thought that it was something of a buzz-box as the power did not come in until pretty high rpm. Nevertheless, during its comparatively brief existence, the 'Triple Knocker' not only provided AJS with a TT victory, but with no less than 21 world records at Montlhéry, the riders being Rod Coleman, Bill Doran and Pierre Monneret, son of the famous Georges Monneret. The young Frenchman took the hour record, and also set up new figures for 50 and 100 kilometres and 50 and 100 miles.

The machine was run without the benefit of any form of streamlining whatsoever, and to reach maximum speed on the undulating and bumpy track the riders had to adopt weird positions to keep out of the air-stream. All three were battered around, and finished the successful attempts stiff and sore. Young Pierre had to be lifted bodily from the machine and given massage treatment before he could even walk.

Jack Williams did not altogether approve of the complicated method of operating the valves, although he welcomed the generous air-space around the exhausts by reason of the longitudinally located camshafts. He did a certain amount of work on the head before concentrating entirely on the 7R, with which he was convinced he could obtain equally good results without the complications and probably better volumetric efficiency. As events proved he was probably right—but Jack Williams is usually right when it comes to motorcycle power-units!

Another version of the three-valve idea was projected for 1955, but this came to naught. Details were released in April 1955, and this time the valves were to be operated by an elaborate system of bevels and pinions, dispensing with the traditional chain method. Styled the 7R3B (presumably the older engine had become 7R3A), it never came out of the experimental shops.

The AMC directors had studied the possibility of producing the 7R3A in series, but were rather frightened off by the construction and tooling estimates. A 'Triple Knocker' would have had splendid publicity value, especially to combat the Norton 'Double Knocker', but that was as far as it was permitted to go. A great deal of money had been spent on the 'Porcupines', without having any tangible results to show for these ingenious machines. AJS would have to get along with what equipment they already possessed.

22: *Jimmy Simpson putting up a record lap at 64.54 mph in the 1924 Junior TT, which was even faster than the same year's Senior record. This machine had the magneto behind the engine.*

23: *In 1921 the $2\frac{3}{4}$ hp Model B had a diamond-shaped frame. By 1925, the only changes were a more vertical saddle down-tube and side sprung (Drew's patent) AJS forks.*

The A.J.S. $2\frac{3}{4}$ h.p. Three-Speed Touring Model B.

24: *Champion of Europe, Jimmy Simpson on the 1923 version (front-magneto) of the 'Big Port', with which he won the European Speed Championships (350 cc) at Monza. He averaged 71 mph, with fastest lap at 76 mph.*

41

25: *Close-up of the 1926 498 cc Model G8, the first overhead valve '500' AJS. The cylinder-head steady bars were fitted a year earlier on the '350'.*

26: *Jimmy Simpson, with George Rowley in the 'chair', during their spectacular ride to finish fifth overall in the 1925 Sidecar TT—with a '350'!*

27: *A 1927 'big single', the 498 cc side-valve Model HP, which was extremely popular as a side-car machine during the late 1920s.*

28: *Last appearance of factory push-rod machines was in the 1928 Senior TT. Here is Jimmy Simpson (above) at Ballacraine making fastest lap at 67.94 mph. George Rowley was second on a similar model.*

29: *Wal Handley (above) on the 349 overhead camshaft AJS. He finished second on this machine in the 1929 Junior TT. The 'cammies' first appeared on the Isle of Man in 1927 but in 1928 push-rod machines were used.*

30: *The AJS works team with the ohc Senior TT machine. From left to right, Leo Davenport, Frank Longman, Tommy Spann, Ronnie Parkinson and George Rowley. Wal Handley is missing from the group.*

31: *Leo Davenport on the 1930 'cammy' model with which he finished tenth in the Junior TT. Apart from fork dampers, it showed little change from the 1929 models.*

32: *For 1934, the 'cammy' machine was considerably altered. The magneto was located behind the more powerful engine and centre-spring forks were adopted. This is the 498 cc machine.*

33: *AJS returned to racing under the Colliers' management in the 1934 TT. Here is that great all-rounder, George Rowley, who finished 12th on his Senior model.*

34: *Jimmy Guthrie, near Keppel Gate, on his 1930 Senior 'cammy'. Earlier he had won the Lightweight TT on the 250 cc version of the overhead camshaft machine.*

35: *The 1929 overhead camshaft model M7 sold at £62 with 349 cc engine and dry-sump lubrication. It was virtually unchanged for 1930 but all-black finish was standardised.*

36: *A twin-port engine was made available for 1929. This is the ohv 498 cc Model M which sold for £62. It weighed 312 lb. and could be supplied with close or wide ratio gearbox. A sloping engine version was added for 1930.*

37: *The 1939 water-cooled version of the four-cylinder model at Brooklands prior to the TT. The additional springs of the forks, hand-adjusted dampers, comparatively wide radiators, supercharger, and projecting oil tank, can be clearly seen.*

38: *Brooklands 'cans' did not add to the general appearance of the 1939 'four'. Fortunately they were discarded for the TT. For a 30-year-old design the 500 cc AJS can stand comparison with many modern racing machines.*

39: *Jock West with the water-cooled 'four' in the 1939 Grand Prix of Belgium. The chain-drive to the supercharger and front-brake torque-arm should be noted.*

40: *Bob Foster (AJS 'four') in the 1939 Senior TT, in which he finished 13th. On this machine Walter Rusk achieved the first 100 mph lap in the Ulster Grand Prix.*

41: *Successful record attempts in 1948 with the 'Porcupine'. Les Graham is just pushing off for his stint, watched by Jock West.*

42: *First appearance of the 'Porcupine' during practice for the 1947 Senior TT. Also possibly the first use of the now-universal face-mask!*

43: *Les Graham rushing down Bray Hill on a 'Porcupine' in the 1949 Senior TT—the same year he won the 500 cc Championship of Europe.*

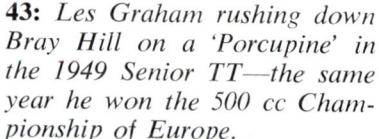

Chapter 6

the 'fours' and the 'porcupine'

NOT THAT the new owners of AJS, H. Collier and Sons Ltd, did not try after they took over in 1931. They were one of the only British manufacturers to see the coming of the 'multis', and to realise the increasing competition which would come from the continent of Europe. They saw Stanley Woods' victory in the 1935 Senior TT on the Guzzi 'twin' as the beginning of a new era. Plumstead also had no illusions about German intentions of using international motorcycle racing for prestige purposes, with BMW, DKW and NSU having as much financial support and encouragement as was being given to the Mercedes-Benz and Auto-Union car-racing concerns in motor car Grands Prix.

The 1935 Motorcycle Show at Olympia provided a major sensation. AJS exhibited a brand-new four-cylinder machine, of striking appearance and with a most advanced specification. Whether or not there were any mechanical parts in the innards was open to question, but the fact remains that the 'four' was a genuine project. Although orders were taken for the machine, none was delivered, and I can find details of only one non-racing machine that was completed and road-tested.

This was an air-cooled, 50 degrees Vee-four of 495 cc (50 × 63 mm) designed by Bert Collier. It was a 4-ohc lay-out, for each cylinder had its own overhead cam-box, driven by chains running up between each pair of cylinders. There were two valves per cylinder head, and four separate exhaust pipes. Two carburettors were employed, bolted to induction pipes running between the two pairs of cylinders. From the offside of the crank-case, bevel gears drove twin magnetos. The frame itself was practically identical to that used for the 'cammy' singles. Transmission was via a Burman four-speed gearbox and the girder forks, wheels and brakes were normal AJS production components.

The exciting 'four' was offered at the attractive price of £89 5s and during the Show the AJS stand was overrun with enthusiasts, potential buyers, and technicians from other factories. Talking point was the provision of an extension to the engine plates, supposedly to locate a dynamo. However, the rumour rapidly gained in strength that the object of this was to permit the mounting of a supercharger.

Whilst conjecture circulated as to the production of the Show model, AJS had already started work on racing editions for 1936. Harold Daniel and George Rowley rode two of the new 'fours' in the 1936 Senior TT, but without any luck. The big machines showed a marked reluctance to remain on four cylinders, and at times resisted all attempts to start their engines.

The project was dropped for 12 months, but the machine reappeared in 1938 with forced induction. Again it was a failure. Power was wasted in driving the supercharger, and serious overheating led to all sorts of troubles. On the straight it was extremely rapid, but completely lacked the acceleration essential to negotiate the tortuous and hilly Island circuit.

Development of the 'four' was then passed to Matt Wright who scrapped the air-cooled engine and had a water-cooled version constructed. A Zoller supercharger had a pressure of 19-20 psi and, on the bench, the engine gave 55 bhp at 7,200 rpm, with a maximum bmep of 200 psi at 7,500 rpm on a compression ratio of 7.9 to 1. Scarcely what one would describe as a 'torquey' unit, but with over 100 bhp per litre, at what appeared to be within fairly safe rpm, Wright and his men were fairly satisfied.

Experiments resulted in the discovery that the most useful top-gear ratio was 4.54 to 1. Installed in a new spring-frame, the engine was a much better proposition than the original 1935 air-cooled unit. However, handling was by no means ideal, in fact at times the father and mother of wobbles was experienced, and the sight of Walter Rusk dashing down Bray Hill in practice was sufficient to make strong men flinch.

There were many problems with cylinder-head gaskets which delayed operations during practice. These were finally overcome but, by the time this was achieved, comparatively few laps had been covered. Rusk did manage to finish 11th, and Bob Foster, on a similar model, was 13th.

It was in that year's Ulster Grand Prix that the 'four' showed its true potential. Rusk, seemingly taking incredible risks to keep the model on the 'tarmac', led the race right from the start, piling on a considerable lead from Freddie Frith (Norton) and Serafini (Gilera 'four'). The 'Blonde Bombshell' became the first man to lap the circuit at 100 mph, and the Ajay folk were understandably

A unique fully exploded drawing by 'Motor Cycle' artist Vic Berris of the famed parallel-twin 'Porcupine' engine. The four-speed gearbox was in unit with the engine and was driven by spur gears. The crankshaft was machined from a solid steel forging, supported in the centre by a plain bearing and by rollers at each end. The con-rods were of forged RR 56 light-alloy construction. Spur gears drove the twin overhead camshafts. Valve-spring wells were contained within the light-alloy cylinder head, which was notable for the spike finning.

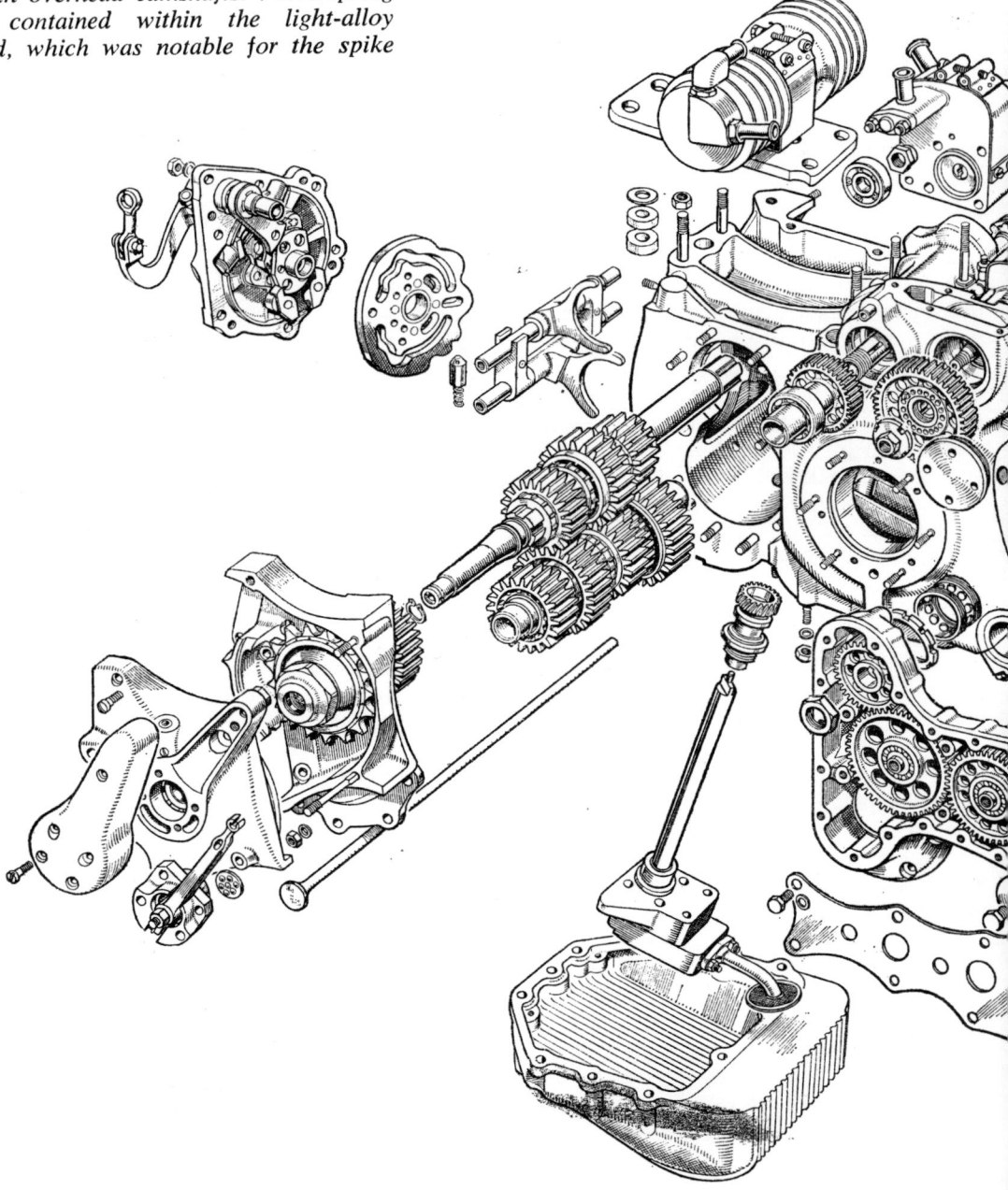

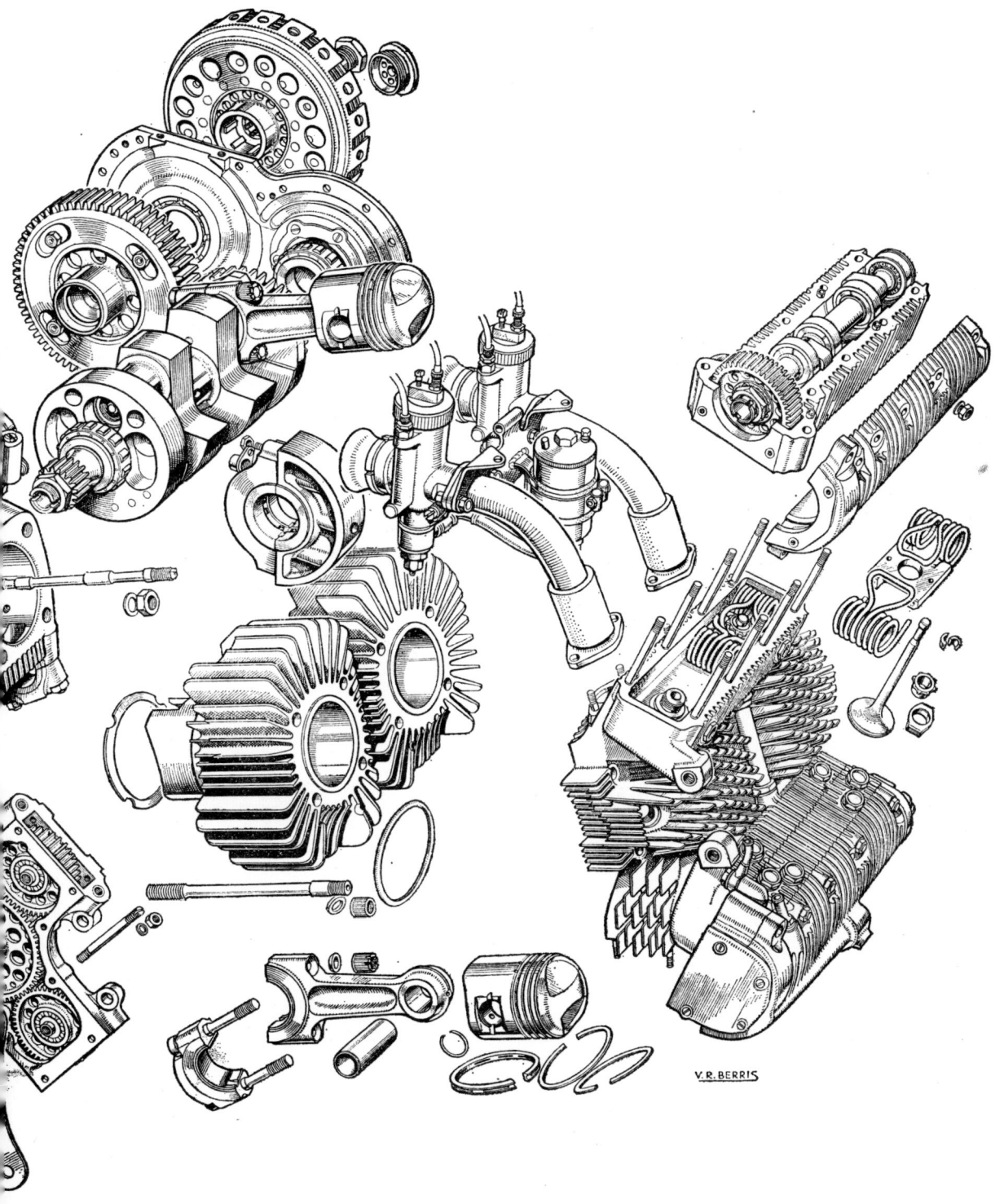

V.R. BERRIS

cock-a-hoop. This was on the third lap but, on the following tour, the front forks broke. People who watched that race maintained that Rusk, using sheer strength to keep the AJS on the road, had caused the links to fracture. Walter appeared to take the difficult handling for granted; his main criticism was that the machine was not fast enough, and when he learned that more power could be produced by stepping up the super-charger-drive ratio, he pestered Matt Wright to 'get some more puff'.

The sight and sound of that supercharged AJS 'four' will never be forgotten. The formula to defeat the German, Swedish and Italian 'multis' was near to realisation but, with the advent of the Second World War, no further development work could be carried out.

During the 'Phoney War' period, Harry Collier and his draughtsmen developed a three-cylinder engine, with separate chain-drive to the three overhead camshafts; it was also designed for forced induction, and the intention was to lay this power-unit, with its parallel cylinders, horizontally in the frame, with the blower and induction located below the petrol tank. What happened to this project remains wrapped in mystery, for when the factory returned to production of peace-time machines an entirely new parallel-twin was in being. This was the famous 'Porcupine', surely the most unlucky machine ever to be raced!

Originally planned for a supercharger, the engine had to be run with normal aspiration, owing to the FIM's decision to ban forced induction in international events. So AJS went over to the Isle of Man for the 1947 Senior TT with Les Graham and Jock West as riders.

As an engineering exercise the parallel-twin was an exquisite piece of work. The engine itself lay practically horizontal in the duplex frame and breaking away from AJS tradition, the two overhead camshafts were driven by a train of spur gears. The cylinder barrels were of 'spiky' construction as regards finning which made the nickname 'porcupine' inevitable. The barrels were of bi-metal construction and the cylinder heads made of light alloy, the camshafts being located across the heads and contained in heavily finned, light-alloy boxes. A most unusual feature was that the engine ran 'backwards'—why this was so, I have never been able to discover, unless someone had theories concerning gyroscopic behaviour when flywheels were permitted to spin the opposite way round. Anyway this entailed drive to the four-speed, close-ratio gearbox by a train of gears. Swing-link rear suspension was adopted, and

the very efficient 'Teledraulic' forks employed.

Of practically square dimensions, the engine was of 499 cc (68 × 68.5 mm). There were quite a number of problems to be overcome, but as the machines were never left out on the circuit at any time during practice for that 1947 Senior event, few people suspected this. Jimmy Simpson, now of course retired as a rider but fully active with the Shell concern, tried everything he knew to gain access to the AJS garage but the 'Porcs' were being worked on in secret. One serious trouble was that the all-fabric clutch plates would not stand up to the power of the engine, and metal plates with Ferodo inserts had to be fabricated on the mainland and rushed over.

Sparking plugs were another major problem. The mica insulation of the plugs then in universal use quickly failed. Eventually this was to lead to the introduction of the very first 'ceramics' sparking plugs designed exclusively by Lodge for the 'Porc' engine.

During practice Jock West had a somewhat frightening experience. When the engines had been run on the bench at Plumstead, Jock mentioned to Bert Collier, the designer, that on full throttle the unit appeared to lift from its mountings. He won-

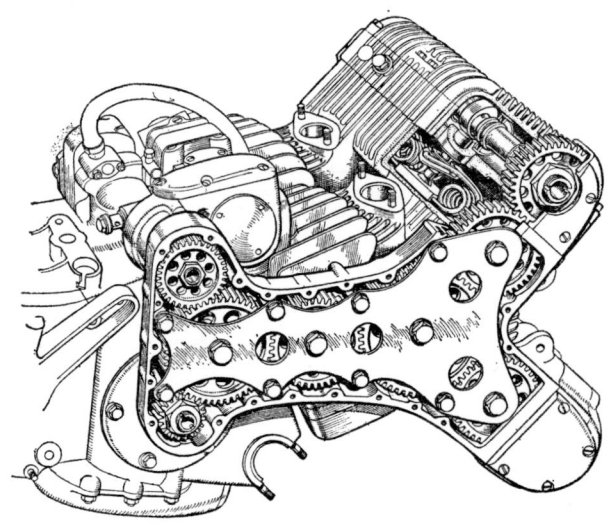

AJS 'Porcupine': The spindles for the camshaft drive pinions were supported in an outrigger plate. The duplex oil pump and magneto were driven from the gear which meshed with the crankshaft half-time pinion. 'Motor Cycle'.

dered what would happen when the power-unit was installed in the frame!

Near the Hawthorns, West suddenly felt everything going haywire. The grass banks were rushing towards him at what seemed to be tremendous velocity. He was fully under the impression that the engine had broken away from the frame. Just as he was picking the softest place to come off, he found that the right-hand section of the light-alloy handlebars had snapped off and that the twist-grip was stuck in the 'full-out' position. His reactions must have been lightning quick, for he managed to pull up the broken bar, shut off the twist-grip, and somehow or other scraped round without falling off. He mentions casually that riding the 'Porc' back to Douglas with only half a handlebar was not one of his most enjoyable trips.

The face-mask used by racing motorcyclists and car men could quite well have been invented by Jock West. Travelling at around two miles a minute when it rained push-rods on the Mountain was not West's idea of a comfortable ride, so he cut out the felt lining from a hat and wrapped it round the lower half of his face. His team-mate Les Graham envied him the mask, so he followed suit, but cut his out from some old green baize from a billiards cloth. Neither cared for the smell of the materials, so they saturated them with some cheap scent. Jock says that the stink of violets stayed on Les' mask for over two years!

The 'one-lunger' brigade was inclined to scoff at the 'Porcs', but after Les Graham finished eighth and Jock West 14th the critics began to sit up and take notice. Both had experienced cutting-out due to the plug insulation becoming overheated and cracking, but when the engines were on two cylinders the machines were very fast indeed. Both West and Graham denied that the 'Porcs' were difficult to handle. It was true that they looked as though they were a handful, so much so that a Belgian rider at Chimay remarked: 'Zig-Ziguant, zey are'.

Harold Wolsey of Lodge produced the promised 'ceramic' plugs, and so confident were West and Graham that they would win at Comminges, they tossed up for who should take the chequered flag. Graham that they would win at Comminges, they a sudden complete cutting-out near the end of the race, wiggled the twist-grip, and then the engine came on to one cylinder and that is how he crossed the line in second place. The mysterious trouble was traced to small cracks which had developed in the ceramic portion, causing a breakdown in the insulation. Rushing along with a dead engine allowed the damaged section to cool off, and

restored the insulation temporarily. Lodge produced much-improved ceramics for later races and these sparking plugs gave no further trouble.

In the 1948 TT the team comprised Les Graham, Jock West and Ted Frend, but all three 'Porcs' failed to finish. However, they did much better elsewhere. West was second in the Belgian GP and third in Holland, while Graham was third in the Ulster GP. In the latter, the team was up against it for scrutineering as all three machines were being worked on. After repeated shouts for the AJS team to weigh-in, Jock West finally dashed up with his mount. It was passed OK and he was asked about the others because time was running out. Jock told the officials that they were on their way, knowing full well that the two machines were in pieces.

Back he went to the garage, whipped his number off, and substituted Graham's. Les duly went to the weigh-in and was passed. The process was repeated with Frend, so everyone seemed to be satisfied. It was rather like Fangio qualifying the entire Maserati team at a certain Grand Prix motor race by judiciously switching cars and numbers!

AJS were determined to win the Senior TT in 1949. Jock West was in charge of operations and the trio comprised Les Graham, Bill Doran and Ted Frend. The machines had been greatly improved and were said to be producing more power than ever before. Apart from Norton and Velocette fans, everyone hoped for a 'Porcupine' win.

On race day, Graham and Frend immediately shot into the lead, the 'Porcs' emitting a thrilling exhaust note that seemed to sound a victory tune —for the first couple of laps at any rate. Then Bob Foster forced the red Guzzi twin in front with a lap of just on 90 mph, pursued by the three Ajays. The Nortons and Velos were being outpaced, so it was developing into a stern battle of the 'multis'.

Then Frend caught a packet on the fourth lap and had to abandon with a twisted frame, bent handlebars and other irreparable broken bits, leaving Les Graham to fight it out with the red Italian machine and Harold Daniell's Norton, then in third place. Graham pushed Foster to such an extent that Bob over-taxed his engine and came to a grinding halt on the sixth lap. Nothing, it seemed, could prevent a 'Porcupine' victory. Alas, Fortune decreed otherwise. Approaching Hilberry, with less than two miles to go and with a two minutes lead over Daniell, the parallel-twin expired. A disconsolate Graham set off to push the heavy machine to the finish, just as Cyril Williams had done so long ago. Rider after rider hurtled past, including Daniell whose Norton engine sounded a trifle rough, but not rough enough to prevent him from taking the chequered flag. It was the bespectacled rider's last TT victory—and decidedly his luckiest!

An exhausted Graham finally struggled home in tenth place behind Doran who was eighth. It had been a bitter disappointment, but such is motor-cycle racing. Anyway Les had the consolation of going on to win the European 500 cc Champion-ship with a victory in the Swiss GP and runner-up in the Ulster. This, at any rate, did vindicate the 'Porcupine'.

AJS had gambled heavily on the TT—and lost. The 'Porcupine' had the reputation of being tem-peramental, and something of a bitch to handle. This was emphatically denied by the trio of riders, and Plumstead still soldiered on. Yet the machines became more and more of an expensive liability;

a sole crumb of comfort, as regards TT aspira-tions, was when Bill Doran finished second to Geoff Duke's Norton in the 1951 Senior. In 1952, the 'Porcupine' was re-designed, and the engine re-located to incline forwards at an angle of 45 degrees to provide a shorter wheelbase. Handling improved considerably and in the 1953 Senior Rod Coleman finished fourth behind the Nortons of Ray Amm and Jack Brett and Reg Armstrong's Gilera 'four'.

That, briefly, is the story of the 'Porcupines'—a courageous effort which just failed to come off in an era when British manufacturers were still com-placent enough to race 'singles' without a thought of what the future might hold. AJS blazed a trail which deserved a more rewarding fate.

Chapter 7

the riders

NO MATTER HOW GOOD a machine may be, success will never come without skilful riders. Down the years, many famous men have been in the saddle of Ajays, contributing each in their way to a share of AJS history. Only Norton can claim to have had a greater number of riders and machines in the TT races. Again, Norton has been represented in every TT week since 1907; AJS began in 1911, skipped 1912 and 1932 and have not missed another since. The marque has scored seven outright victories, innumerable placings, and has twice lifted the hard-won manufacturers' award.

Naturally, as a full personality parade would occupy many pages, I propose merely to refer to the better-known riders in each era. Therefore let's start with Howard R. Davies, the only man ever to win a Senior TT riding a 350 cc machine. Still in his teens, Howard Davies began his motorcycling career in 1911 riding Sunbeams for the designer, J. E. Greenwood, who had left JAPs to join John Marston. He continued to ride Sunbeams in every type of speed event and trial, and also showed a distinct aptitude for things mechanical. Given his first ride in the 1914 Senior TT on a Sunbeam, he finished equal second to O. C. Godfrey (Indian) and was credited with a record lap, later annulled owing to a difference of opinion between time-keepers!

He was reported killed in action on the Western Front but, as Mark Twain once remarked, 'The report of my death was an exaggeration'. After demob, he joined A. J. Stevens and Co Ltd as tester and rider; his first TT race for the factory was in 1920 on the then revolutionary ohv '350'. When disputing the lead with Eric Williams mechanical bothers intervened and he had to retire. The tubby Welshman, with his Charlie Chaplin moustache, was a glutton for work. His mechanical knowledge made him invaluable to the Stevens brothers, and he put in countless hours at Brooklands in all sorts of weather.

After his wonderfully successful 1921 efforts he did even more testing, mainly during the development of the 'big port'. He rode in events whenever possible, and again for AJS in both Senior and Junior TTs in 1922 and 1923, but retired on all four occasions. He quit AJS in 1924 to design, build and ride his own machine—the very handsome and effective HRD with which he was second

in the 1925 Junior. Using the latest JAP racing two-port engine he also won the Senior in 1925. He retired from racing in 1927 and joined up with Phil Vincent to construct the sprung-frame Vincent-HRD. Howard Davies was an exceptionally brilliant rider and could truthfully be said to have been the first AJS 'star'.

Eric and Cyril Williams, who were not related, did sterling work for AJS in the years prior to, and immediately after, the First World War. Despite Eric's two victories, Cyril Williams is remembered more because of that epoch-making effort in 1920, when he manhandled his crippled machine about four miles to the finish—and still won!

AJS never had a character quite like Jimmy Simpson, the greatest favourite the Manx crowds ever had. 'Jimmy the S' had just one idea and that was to go faster than anyone else. A highly spectacular rider, he was of the same tough school that produced 'iron men' like Freddie Dixon and Rhodesia's Ray Amm. During his 13 years career, Jimmy took part in 26 TTs but finished in only 11 of them. However he set up eight lap records and won just one race — the 1934 Lightweight on a Rudge. As well as being the first rider to do 60 mph and 70 mph laps (both on Ajays), he was the first to attain 80 mph, which he did in 1930 on a Senior Norton.

Simpson started riding in the Island in 1922 on a Scott, then on Ajays until 1928, and after that all Nortons except for his winning Lightweight race. He never lived down a reputation of being an engine-buster and it is said that, in their efforts to keep pace with the Simpson trail of exploded power-units, the Stevens brothers built into their machines the added reputation for reliability that carried the marque on for many years. He was a legend of his time and, at the start of every one of his races, the betting usually was that 'Simpson is bound to pull it off this time'. After he gave up professional riding he became 'Mr Shell' in the motorcycle-racing sphere and, following many years with the oil company, retired to the West Country where he lives, surrounded by the countless reminders of his racing days.

Jimmy Guthrie from Hawick, Scotland, was a motorcycling 'great' who won no less than six TT races including the Lightweight in 1930 on an AJS 'cammy'. Jim had his first TT ride in 1923 on a

Matchless. He did not reappear in the Island until 1927 when he showed his mettle by taking second place in the Senior on a New Hudson. From then on, until he lost his life in that tragic crash in the German Grand Prix in 1937, 'Jimmy the G' rode only Norton or AJS. In 1931, he won two TT races in the same week, then the third rider to do so. He was involved in what must have been one of the closest TTs of all time when, after being hailed as the winner on his Norton, he had to abdicate in favour of Stanley Woods who, during a record-smashing last lap on the big twin-cylinder Guzzi, won by precisely four seconds. That was a race that I shall never forget! There is a memorial to Jimmy Guthrie on Snaefell near the spot where he retired during the 1937 Senior—his last TT.

Wal Handley was another rider who won two TTs in the same week, but this time in 1925. He also established record laps in both these races and, for good measure, did the same in the Lightweight — a feat which no other rider has ever equalled.

He was just 18 years old when he started his career in 1922, making fastest lap in his very first TT; his OK-Blackburne was five mph quicker than the 1920 lap record. His main successes were on that now defunct make, the Rex-Acme, but he was second on a 'cammy' Ajay in the 1929 Junior. During a career which lasted 13 years and 28 TTs, he always reckoned that the AJS was the most pleasant of all the machines he rode. He took up car racing and lost his life during the Second World War when his transport plane crashed.

Harold Daniell came to racing via the Manx GP after winning the 1933 Senior. He was quickly signed up as an AJS works rider but was somewhat unlucky with the ohc machines, doing no better than an eighth and a ninth in the Junior. In 1936, he rode the sensational AJS supercharged 'four' but had to retire with mechanical troubles. A quiet, unassuming, bespectacled Londoner, Harold was the first man to cover the Isle of Man circuit in under 25 minutes, which he did in 1938 at an average speed of 91 mph. He won the 1947 and 1949 Seniors for Norton and retired from motorcycle racing in 1951. He turned to 500 cc car racing, but with moderate success, and became a popular performer at Brands Hatch, sometimes in a front-drive Emeryson. He also sponsored Mike O'Rourke on an Ariel Arrow. Harold Daniell died in 1967 after a brief illness.

Like Guthrie, Bob McIntyre was a Scot. His name will always be coupled with those of Geoff Duke, John Surtees and Mike Hailwood as a 'top tiger'. It was Bob McIntyre who achieved the first

magic 100 mph TT lap (actually 101.12 mph) in 1957 on a Gilera. After a splendid debut in 1952, when he finished second in the Clubman's TT and set fastest lap, he returned the following year for the Manx Grand Prix with a 7R AJS and promptly won the Junior. Not only that, but he almost did a Howard Davies by taking second place on the same machine in the Senior.

Mac became a member of the AJS team, for whom he put up many splendid rides, but from 1954 onwards the foreign challenge was on with a vengeance and he did not have a lot of luck. He did, however, have some excellent results with a Joe Potts-tuned 7R after AJS quit racing in 1956. To the dismay of his countless friends and admirers, Bob lost his life in an accident at Oulton Park in 1962.

Mike Hailwood's remarkable career embraced many races on a 7R, a type which was one of his favourites, especially for short-circuit racing. He did not manage to finish the two TTs he entered with the 'Boys' Racer' in 1960 and 1961. In the latter event, victory was snatched from him on the very last lap when a gudgeon pin broke with only 13 miles to go. When this happened, he was out on his own and no-one had a hope of catching him.

Les Graham, Bill Lomas, Ted Frend, Walter Rusk, Jock West, Rod Coleman, Alastair King and Alan Shepherd were all first-rate riders with many AJS successes to their credit. Graham, especially, had the most wretched luck; his 'Porcupine' broke down just two miles from the finish when he was leading the 1949 Senior and, like Hailwood a couple of years later, he had the race in his pocket. It was a sad day for the sport when he lost his life after an inexplicable crash going down Bray Hill on an MV in 1953.

Coleman, a most stylish rider, won the 1954 Junior on his 7R3 and scored the first AJS TT victory since Guthrie's 1930 success. Bill Doran had the best Isle of Man result with a 'Porcupine', finishing second to Geoff Duke's Norton in the 1951 Senior. Walter Rusk was a highly spectacular rider without an atom of fear in his make-up. He took the difficult AJS 'four' in his stride, frightening everyone except himself. Rusk was a great lover of big, powerful machines and was the first to do a 100 mph lap in the Ulster Grand Prix, riding the Ajay 'four'. Ted Frend had many fine results during his five years with AJS and was one of the 'Porc' trio. Alastair King won the one and only Formula One race in the Isle of Man on his 7R, as well as having a colourful career on various makes of machine from 1957 to 1963. The same could be said of Alan Shepherd who, from 1959 to 1964, always seemed to be more at home on a 'Boys' Racer' than on anything else.

Jock West, now an executive with Glanfield Lawrence Ltd, was a great asset to the Colliers in the development of the 7R, and also in racing the 'Porcupines'. Perhaps better known as one of the fastest of the supercharged BMW riders, Jock is one of motorcycling's real personalities. Geoff Murdoch, until recently competitions manager of Esso, took 4th place in the 1948 Senior TT.

Mike Duff has ridden both 7R and the very special Arter edition with great verve. He per-

severed with Arter's re-vamped 'Porc' a few years ago, but the Ajay was plainly outclassed by more modern machinery. Bob Foster, when he rode for AJS, was not exactly blessed with good fortune, particularly with the 'four'.

One could go on and on, but I think that this chapter will give the reader some idea of the big names that AJS has commanded. It may be thought that I have overlooked George Rowley who rode Ajays in no less than 19 TTs. However the great all-rounder has plenty of space devoted to him in the Trials chapter.

Chapter 8

AJS and trials

WHEN ONE THINKS of trials in relation to AJS one naturally conjures up the names of George Rowley, Hugh Viney, Gordon Jackson and Bob Manns. It was that great all-rounder Rowley who established the reputation of the marque in arduous six-day events. He provided a professional approach which was in direct contrast to the somewhat haphazard entries in the scores of reliability trials held up and down the country in the early days.

George Rowley was equally at home in races, scrambles, speed hill-climbs and trials. Without being a 'tiger', he had a fine road-racing record both in Great Britain and abroad, with a second place in the 1928 Senior TT and many victories in continental events. From 1925 until he retired from competitive riding in 1939 he rode exclusively for AJS and was directly concerned in the testing and development of many projects. When Colliers took over the company in 1931, Rowley moved to Plumstead and was involved at once in a rigorous programme of testing and developing prototypes at Brooklands. He was told by Harry Collier—'no racing', but he still managed to compete in the odd trial and, as related, was directly responsible for the re-entry of AJS into racing when the Colliers decided to re-introduce the 'cammy' model.

Rowley's record in the long-distance 'classics' was most impressive. To that must be added a long list of successes in one-day and half-day sporting trials. He was completely dedicated and absolutely meticulous (even fussy) when it came to the preparation of his machines. He would experiment with various shapes of cam and different weights of flywheel to obtain maximum torque at low engine speeds which suited his method of 'trickling' up muddy and rocky sections. His influence on trials 'irons' in general was considerable and he doubtless communicated his ideas to those riders who followed him after the Second World War.

He was extremely popular with the motorcycling press. *The Motor Cycle* described him as being: 'easily the most skilful and polished rider in trials, who makes the most terrifying of sections look absurdly simple. The turn-out of his AJS machines is immaculate, and is a feature of the entire AJS team. He seems to be able to adapt his riding to any sort of condition and weather, and must surely have fewer mechanical break-downs than anyone else'.

The comments of *Motor Cycling* were: 'A magnificent rider, always fast, effortless and sure: probably the most spectacular rider in the trial (the 1929 'Scottish') and certainly the most popular with spectators'.

Rowley had a sure eye for promising riders. One of his discoveries was Leo Davenport, who was with AJS from 1928 to 1930, and rode in several races as well as trials eventually winning the 1932 Lightweight TT on a New Imperial. C. E. Wise was another racing man who played a strong supporting role in trials, assisting AJS to carry off many manufacturers' team trophies.

George Rowley was selected for the first time as a member of the British International Six Days Trophy Team in 1929, riding a 349 cc ohv AJS. The previous week he had won the 350 cc Austrian Grand Prix, going straight on to compete in the ISDT which, that year, was the stiffest event so far organised. Starting in Munich and finishing at Geneva, the route passed through Germany, Austria, France and Italy. Rowley, unfamiliar with the terrain, put up a remarkable performance on his little AJS and did not lose a single penalty mark. With F. W. 'Freddie' Neill (Matchless) and G. R. Butcher (Rudge-Whitworth s/c), he won the Trophy for Great Britain, holders in 1912 and from 1924 to 1928.

An example of George Rowley's skill was on a 1 in 3 'terror' near Oberau, where practically the entire entry failed. The AJS rider picked his way up delicately to the top non-stop, while others were pushing and shoving, many abandoning their machines in disgust. The route was littered with motorcycles, and how the British rider successfully made the climb dumbfounded the continentals. With Davenport and Wise, the AJS trio lifted the 350 cc Manufacturers' Trophy.

As soon as this arduous event had been completed, Davenport and Rowley were off to the Ulster Grand Prix where they finished first and second in the 350 cc category on their 'cammy' Ajays.

A truly remarkable man, he continued at Plumstead when the company was taken over by AMC and, after the War, must be given the credit for much of the development of that most successful of all trials motorcycles, the 16MC 347 cc AJS. From 1946 he directed AJS trials activities until

Hugh Viney was appointed competitions manager in 1949. His vast experience was invaluable, not only in selecting the most suitable types of machine, but also in spotting likely material.

During the golden days of AJS activities in trials, embracing the period from 1947 to 1962, there was no brighter star than Hugh Viney who had competed in pre-war events with moderate success, mostly on a modified 'big port'. Just as Hugh was becoming better known the War intervened, and he spent much of the 'phoney' period as a despatch rider instructor for the Royal Corps of Signals. The Army could not have made a more fortuitous choice, and many a young recruit received valuable basic instruction in the art of rough-riding on WD machines in the Catterick area.

Hugh Viney himself was determined to become a works rider and in 1946 he badgered George Rowley to lend him a '350' for the Beggars' Roost Trial. George was more than impressed with the stylish and effortless riding of this unassuming young man and, following several successful outings, persuaded the AMC managing director, Mr D. S. Heather, to take him on as a factory rider at Plumstead. This was in March 1947, and Hugh had no compunction about reporting for duty on All Fools Day !

The confidence that Rowley had in his young protégé was soon vindicated. One month after joining AJS, Viney, on a '350', won the extremely rough and tough Scottish Six Days Trial with the loss of only six penalty points. No rider, before or since (apart from the very first event, of course), had ever succeeded in winning the 'Scottish' at a first attempt. The experienced Scottish officials had thought up the most devilish course possible but Viney treated even the worst sections as if they did not exist.

In 1948, even more 'impossible' stuff was included, and once again Hugh Viney made best performance, dropping only 27 points, when much more experienced riders were collecting penalties amounting to three figures. This event was run during petrol rationing, but a special dispensation from the Ministry of Fuel permitted the trial to be staged as it was considered vital to the development of post-war machines.

Hugh's brilliant performance led to a place in the British Trophy Team for the ISDT. Again riding his favourite 350 cc AJS, he went through the entire six days without dropping a single mark, and helped the team to win the Trophy. Not long afterwards he won the very sticky Southern Experts Trial.

Success followed success. Hugh Viney (AJS) became the most difficult rider to beat in any of the trade-supported events. Then, in 1949, he achieved the unprecedented feat of winning the 'Scottish' for the third successive year. Mr J. R. Alexander, who had presented the massive silver trophy, offered him the choice of keeping it, or having a cheque and a replica—Hugh chose the latter. He had lost 18 marks, eight less than his nearest competitor.

Once again he was in the ISDT Trophy team. The 1949 event was staged in Wales, and Great Britain won for the second year running with Viney and his AJS remaining unpenalised. He won the 'Southern Experts' again and, shortly afterwards, took over the job of competitions manager to AJS.

For 1950, he was joined by P. J. Mellers and T. H. Wortley, the latter replacing C. A. Mein, who had moved to Douglas. Mellers later left the team and A. W. Burnand took his place.

That was the year that Hugh Viney did not win the 'Scottish', but he was runner-up to another AMC rider, 'Artie' Ratcliffe on a Matchless. A measure of his fame was that, in reporting the event, the headlines in a Scottish newspaper read: 'Viney defeated at last !' For the third successive year he made an unpenalised run in the ISDT, Great Britain again winning the Trophy. Viney, Wortley and Burnand took the coveted Manufacturers' Award for AJS.

In the 1951 Scottish Six Days Trial Hugh won a first-class award, but for once he had mechanical troubles. A slipping clutch and a broken chain lost him marks on vital sections. However, once again he had an unpenalised run in the ISDT and was a member of the winning Trophy team as well as the AJS/Matchless entry in the Manufacturers' contest.

Viney collected yet another first-class award in the 1952 'Scottish', with a new AJS team-rider, Gordon Jackson, third overall. Hugh captained the British Trophy team in the ISDT, this time riding a '500'. However, despite some brilliant riding by the AJS man, Great Britain could do no better than third place.

In 1953, Hugh Viney (347 AJS) won the 'Scottish' for the fourth time. Bob Manns had now joined the team and, with Viney and Jackson, AJS took the Manufacturers' Award. He returned to a '350' for the ISDT and, as was his habit, dropped not one single mark, captaining the British team which won the Trophy. He was also a member of the AJS/Matchless team which were runners-up in the Manufacturers' Trophy.

The 1954 'Scottish' saw Gordon Jackson again in third place, and another first-class award to Viney who, with Manns and Jackson, again lifted the Manufacturers' Award for AJS. That year, Great Britain was second in the ISDT, Viney again putting up an immaculate display on his '350'.

That formidable trio, Viney, Jackson and Manns (all on 347 cc Ajays), once more took the Manufacturers' Award in the 'Scottish'. Jackson was again third and both Viney and Manns had first-class awards. Not long afterwards the popular AJS competitions manager was involved in a road accident in London from which he received painful leg injuries. The ISDT had lost their brilliant captain and AJS their most valued rider, for it was many months before he was fit again. The loss of Viney was a severe blow to the British Trophy team and it was significant that, for the first time since the post-war series was resumed, the team was completely out of the picture.

Nevertheless the 1956 'Scottish' proved that AJS had yet another star to follow in Viney's saddle. Gordon Jackson, who had been third overall for three successive years, won outright, with Gordon McLaughlin in third place, also on a 347 cc AJS. For the fourth year running, the Manufacturers' Award went to the AJS team (Jackson, Manns and McLaughlin). Jackson had started riding in trials at the age of 16 and joined AJS in 1952. When he won the 'Scottish' he was holder of the ACU Trials Drivers' Star.

That stalwart, Bob Manns, went through the ISDT without dropping a point, but mechanical trouble affecting another team-member dropped Great Britain to third place. Without possessing the sheer brilliance of Viney and Jackson, Manns was a top-line rider, making a major contribution to what continued to be the most powerful manufacturers' trio in trials.

Returning to Jackson, I believe that a brief recap of the 1956 'Scottish' will emphasise the quality of endurance possessed both by the rider and his meticulously prepared AJS 16MC. From the start, Jackson had to fight all the way and having lost a solitary mark on the first day, he was behind four other riders who were 'clean'. The sections were rugged, many of them simply dried-up burns or stone and boulder-strewn tracks. One by one his rivals fell by the wayside as the going became tougher and tougher and, by the half-way stage, Gordon was leading the entry, with only Arthur Lampkin (BSA) and his team-mate Gordon McLaughlin (347 AJS) in a position to challenge him.

Jackson's riding was truly inspired and, in the Viney and Rowley tradition, he 'trickled' his way up the most terrifying sections where others footed and even fell off. It was also a year of mechanical troubles, but not for Jackson, whose 16MC never missed a beat: he went on to score his first major victory in a long-distance event.

Two years later, Jackson again won the 'Scottish' and was runner-up in 1959. Victorious again in 1960, the following year he equalled Hugh Viney's record of four outright wins. In that particular event he put up a truly amazing performance, losing only a single penalty point. This was for a slight 'dab' on the rocky slopes of the notorious Grey Mare's Ridge during an event which was notable for the large number of experts who failed. In 1962, Jackson was runner-up, again on a 16MC.

I feel that the list of AJS successes in the Scottish Six Days Trials ought to be given, for I doubt whether any make or riders will achieve a similar record in such a difficult event. Out of the 16 trials held from 1947 to 1962, Viney and Jackson won eight between them. Viney's hat-trick stands alone, as does a similar feat by the AJS team in the Manufacturers' contest. At a dinner given by the Edinburgh St George MCC in 1961, a speaker referred to the classic event as the 'Viney and Jackson AJS Six Days'. So, for the record, here is the run-down of the AJS achievements:

1947	1st Hugh Viney
1948	1st Hugh Viney
1949	1st Hugh Viney
1950	2nd Hugh Viney
1952	3rd Gordon Jackson
1953	1st Hugh Viney; 3rd Gordon Jackson Manufacturers' Award (Viney, Jackson, Manns)
1954	3rd Gordon Jackson Manufacturers' Award (Viney, Jackson, Manns)
1955	3rd Gordon Jackson Manufacturers' Award (Viney, Jackson, Manns)
1956	1st Gordon Jackson; 3rd Gordon McLaughlin. Manufacturers' Award (Jackson, Manns, McLaughlin)
1958	1st Gordon Jackson
1960	1st Gordon Jackson
1961	1st Gordon Jackson
1962	2nd Gordon Jackson

No matter how good the design and construction of a machine, without the dedicated work put in by the mechanics the finest riders on the best machines would have little in the way of successes. During the 1947-1962 period the preparation of the works Ajays was a byword. The main brunt of the work fell on Wally Wyatt and Charlie

Plummer—two men who could virtually strip, tune and re-assemble a 16MC blind-folded.

They tested and balanced every single component. Ports were polished till they shone like mirrors. They knew which grade of sparking plug would suit any particular type of event. Tuning carburettors was another of their specialities, and no machine was permitted to leave the competitions department at Plumstead until Wyatt and Plummer considered it to be 100 per cent. Anything that was liable to work loose was firmly secured and, when the riders took over, they knew full well that their mounts were absolutely tip-top in every way.

In these days, everyone at Plumstead followed the fortunes of the AJS trials team. Wyatt and Plummer were regarded with the same veneration

as were the team riders and this enthusiasm was communicated throughout the entire factory.

Bob Manns, who is still with the company (now Norton Villiers), recalls the long hours put in by Wyatt, Plummer and their men, with no thought of overtime but merely a burning desire to look after their charges. He also pays tribute to the support which was given to the riders during the arduous six-day events, usually entailing travelling long distances, and sometimes days at a stretch without sleep. Bob continues: 'The debt that is owed to these men should never be forgotten. Without their efforts, AJS participation in trials would never have met with the success it did'.

Although 498 cc models were often used, the mainstay of the AJS onslaught was the 347 cc Model 16, or 16C and later 16MC as it was styled

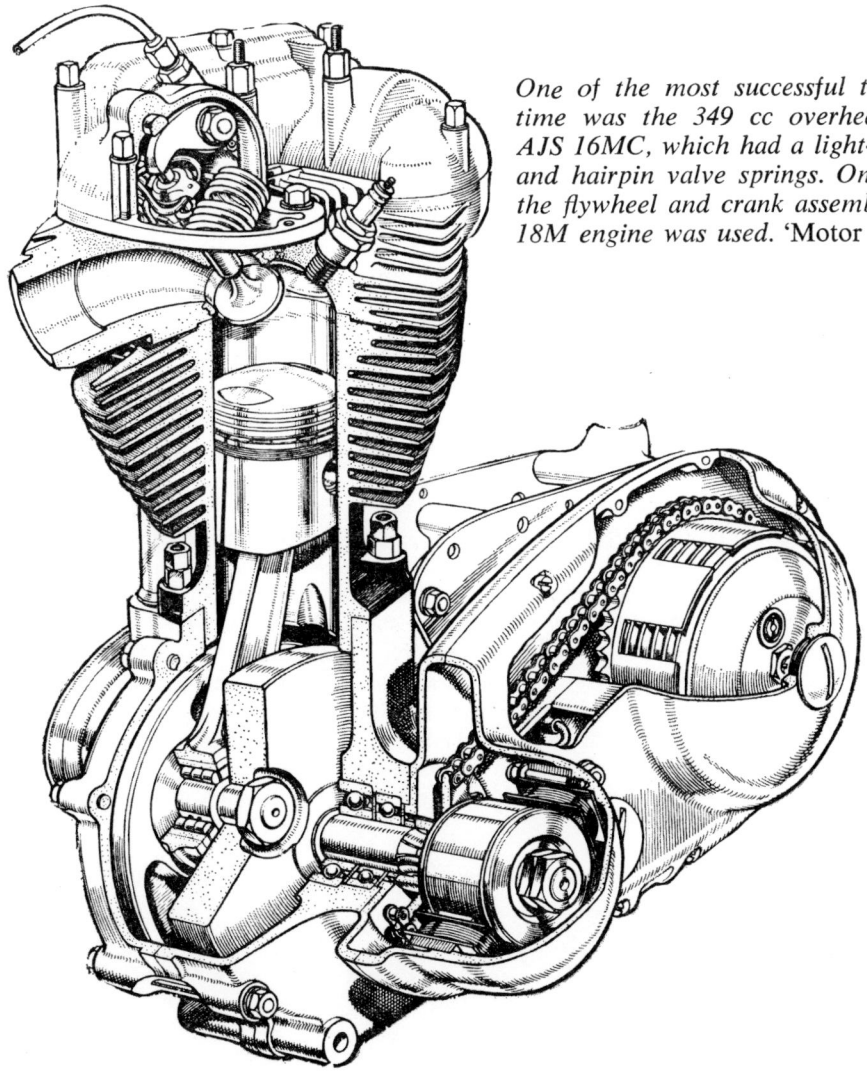

One of the most successful trials engines of all time was the 349 cc overhead-valve (push-rod) AJS 16MC, which had a light-alloy cylinder head and hairpin valve springs. On the works engines the flywheel and crank assembly from the 498 cc 18M engine was used. 'Motor Cycle'.

in competition form. The push-rod engine was of 69 × 93 mm, the long-stroke unit always being considered most suited for trials work. It had a deeply finned, light-alloy cylinder head, which incorporated cast-in valve seats. The stellite-tipped valves were chromium-plated and were operated via a twin, gear-driven cam, hardened steel followers and duralumin push-rods and rockers. Duplex hairpin valve springs were featured and the valve gear, including the guides, was positively lubricated. Finned to match the head, the close-grained iron cylinder was attached to the light-alloy crankcase by four large-diameter nuts and bolts.

Cast-iron flywheels were favoured for the works engines. These were carefully balanced and heavier than those on the standard units. Actually the bottom-end was largely that of the '500', this being found to provide exceptional flexibility at comparatively low rpm. The crankshaft assembly comprised a two-piece crankpin, forged steel con rod, triple-row caged roller bearings for the big end, and hardened steel mainshafts. The crankcase had twin-caged rollers on the drive side and a single, flanged phosphor-bronze bush on the timing side. From the timing side of the mainshaft was driven a duplex, plunger-type rotary reciprocating oil pump, which circulated lubricant to all moving parts from the separate oil tank. The crankcase included a magnetic oil filter; the AC generator was operated from the drive-side mainshaft, and the ignition contact breaker from the inlet camshaft. The Amal carburettor had a choke diameter of $1\frac{1}{16}$ inch. Normally, a 6.5 to 1 compression ratio was employed for trials work.

Transmission was through a multi-plate clutch and four-speed Burman gearbox, later replaced by one of AMC manufacture. A positively operated foot-change was fitted, and the ratios were normally 14.85, 9.85, 7.08, and 5.80 to 1. Engine, clutch, gearbox and rear-wheel sprockets were of 19, 42, 16 and 42 teeth respectively.

The duplex frame was of welded construction whereas that of the production model was brazed. It was made from high-grade steel tubing with malleable iron lugs. Rear suspension was of the swinging-arm pattern with unusually large and robust self-lubricating pivot points. The rubber-bushed, oil-damped suspension units were fixed to the top of the frame on the saddle extension rails. Forks were the well-tried Teledraulic oil-damped units, incorporating special competition springs.

The light-alloy petrol tank held two gallons and the oil tank half-a-gallon. The wheels had specially strengthened heat-treated spindles and carried a 2.75 × 21 inch tyre in front, with a 4.00 × 19 inch at the rear, the latter being provided with security bolts. The mudguards were of light alloy, a steel undershield was fitted to protect the crankcase, and the exhaust pipe was upswept. The frame itself was shorter than that of the standard Model 16, and the machine scaled just 260 lb. By shortening the duplex down-tubes a ten inch ground clearance was obtained.

To suit Gordon Jackson's 'trickle' methods, the AJS mechanics evolved an 'engine-speed' magneto. I understand that this was the first and only mag-drive that was ever used on a trials machine that ran at precisely engine speed.

One must not overlook the many splendid performances put up by Frank Giles in AJS sidecar outfits in the toughest events that organisers could devise; also the feats of Geoff Ward, British Trials Champion and holder of the ACU Gold Star in 1951. Going back even further than before the days of George Rowley, Alec Jackson (550 cc AJS) in 1925 was the first rider to break the domination of Scott-mounted men, in the famous Scott Trial, staged in the wildest of the wild Yorkshire moors. Successes by private owners in every type of trial were legion: as for the International 'Six Days', the ACU owe a great deal to the immaculately prepared AJS machines, and to their superb riders, for upholding British prestige.

This, then, was what must be regarded as the most successful of all trials machines. It would require many, many pages to enumerate the countless successes which were obtained with it in every type of event, from the smallest of club 'half-days' to the major International long-distance affairs. Anyway, I think the achievements of Viney, Jackson, Rowley, Manns, McLaughlin and others speak for themselves.

Chapter 9

the amateur TT and the manx grand prix

WHEN THE AMATEUR ROAD RACES in the Isle of Man were introduced in 1923 the event was styled the Amateur TT and was run over the same circuit as the June races, but in the month of September. Difficulty in maintaining a true amateur status almost caused the races to be abandoned after 1929, but new rules led to their being replaced by what we now know as the Manx Grand Prix. These stipulated that, firstly, the competitors had, at the time of entry, to have been at least five years domiciled in Great Britain, Northern Ireland, the Irish Free State, the Isle of Man or the Channel Islands, and secondly, they must not have either ridden in, or been nominated as a reserve for, any international race since 1920 nor, since the same date, have held any world motorcycle record.

In the early days, the organisers were so afraid of commercialism that any form of race advertising was prohibited and, when public address systems came into use, no mention of the makes of machine was permitted.

AJS had their first Amateur TT victory in 1926 when R. D. Adams won on a 498 cc 'big port' at 58.46 mph and also set fastest lap at 61.76 mph. In these days, both 500 cc and 350 cc classes were lumped together, and it was not until 1928 that separate Senior and Junior events were staged. For the next 12 years, AJS were no longer in the results, successes in the races going to Norton, Excelsior, Velocette, Triumph, Rudge and Guzzi machines. However, in 1948 E. A. Barrett was second on his AJS and another AJS ridden by Reg Armstrong made fastest lap at 79.543 mph.

The Junior races were the main events for AJS riders, for which the 7R 'Boys' Racer' was ideal. It was the type of machine these races had been devised for. Don Crossley was third in 1949 and won the 1950 Junior after a long and close-fought duel with Peter Romaine (Norton). In 1951, it was Robin Sherry's turn to win, averaging 82.61 mph and turning fastest lap at 83.91 mph. Harold Clark was third on another AJS.

The 1952 Senior resulted in victory for Derek Farrant on a Matchless-AJS, with Bob McIntyre second on a pukka 'Boys' Racer'. Farrant won at the remarkable average speed of 88.65 mph, setting up a new Manx GP lap record at 89.64 mph. The Junior was all AJS, the marque taking the first four places, headed by McIntyre, Clark and Farrant. Bob's winning speed was 85.73 mph and Clark set up a new Junior lap record at 87.37 mph. Farrant's performance with the hybrid meant that the race for the first 90 mph lap was on with a vengeance. It is worth considering that 41 Ajays started the race, and 33 finished — a truly fine demonstration of reliability.

Derek Ennett won the 1954 Junior at 86.33 mph, with John Hartle third on another 'Boys' Racer'. Alastair King made the fastest lap at 87.77 mph. In the previous year, the magic '90' had been achieved by Dennis Parkinson (Norton) in the Senior.

Newer and much faster ohc Nortons were made available, and provided the marque with a clean sweep in both Senior and Junior races from 1955 to 1957. It was Alan Shepherd on the Bancroft-AJS who broke the stranglehold of Bracebridge Street by winning the 1958 Junior at 89.08 mph, with the fastest lap at 90.58 mph. The following year, R. C. Ritchie was third in the Junior, whilst Roy Mayhew was runner-up in 1960, with Ron Langston on another AJS returning fastest lap at 91.69 mph.

The 1961 Junior was a sweeping AJS victory, Frank Reynolds being followed home by Rob Dawson and A. Newstead. The race was also a tragedy, for that very promising rider Fred Neville lost his life when his 7R crashed on the last lap when he was in the lead. The weather was atrocious, with heavy rain and high winds. Reynolds' winning speed was down to 81.28 mph and Neville made fastest lap at a mere 85.22 mph, about seven mph below the 1960 figures.

Dawson won the 1962 Junior at 89.02 mph and put the lap record up to 91.87 mph. Peter Darvill took second place on another 7R. In 1963, AJS scored another '1, 2, 3', Darvill winning from Alan Hunter and Selwyn Griffiths at the very high average of 92.48 and with an astonishing fastest lap at 93.87 mph.

Malcolm Uphill (7R) was a close second in the 1964 Junior to David Williams on his MW-Special. He averaged a record 92.54 mph but, oddly enough, Darvill's lap record remained unbroken. However in 1965 George Buchan (Norton) pushed it up to 93.96 mph. Buchan led right up until the last lap when a chain broke, leaving Uphill to win on his AJS at 91.22 mph from Nigel Warren, also

Ajay-mounted. Uphill did the double that year, winning the Senior on a Norton—a feat that had been achieved only once before, by Alan Holmes (Norton) in 1957.

That 1965 Junior had a most exciting climax. Uphill eased off slightly before he started out on his last lap, confident that he had a useful lead. Yet, unknown to him, another AJS had been streaking round the Island with Warren in the saddle. He reduced a 15-second deficit to a three-second lead, a fact that was not transmitted to Uphill by his pit. On the last lap, to his utter astonishment, a supporter waved a chalked board at him near Ballaugh Bridge which read 'Minus 2'. With 20 miles to go, Malcolm suddenly woke up and began motorcycle racing in real earnest. Back at the grandstands on Glencrutchery Road, the PA announcers were almost incoherent. At Ramsey Hairpin, they were level pegging. Both riders took their willing engines up to, and even beyond, peak rpm. Afterwards spectators said that Uphill's progress down the Mountain was heart-stopping. He scraped his footrest at Creg-ny-Baa, then went up through the gears and absolutely harry-flatters to Brandish, after standing on his brakes to take this second-gear corner. Sweeping through the Hilberry right-hander at about 100 mph he then braked hard for Signpost, followed by the Nook, and the tricky Governor's Bridge, which was taken at almost crawling speed in bottom gear. Up through the gears again, and then it was head down and full out to the finish. After that hairy last lap, Uphill won by exactly six seconds. How he must have blessed that spectator at Ballaugh Bridge!

When one realises that the 7R went out of production in 1962 (only a handful were delivered),

the record of the 'Boys' Racer' in the Manx races is all the more remarkable. These events are every bit as important to manufacturers as the June races—particularly if race replicas are listed in the catalogue. The 'pro' races offer quite a different challenge for, nowadays, only specially constructed racing machines stand a chance of winning. Entering a production racer is rather like pitting a hotted-up sports-car against the latest Formula One single-seater in the racing-car world. Fortunately for the peace of mind of Manx entrants few, if any, ex-works racers are ever sold outside the factory and, if they are, they invariably go to specific professionals with the proviso that only they can ride them.

These September races have been the nursery for many world-famous riders. I believe it is worth recording in this chapter the names of some of those who took part in them before embarking on a professional career. They were men such as Reg Armstrong, Tom Arter, Bill Beevers, Charlie Dodson, Austin Munks, Bill Lomas, Geoff Duke, Phil Read, Percy Hunt, Bob McIntyre, 'Crasher' White, Ted Mellors, Harold Daniell, Joe Dunphy, Freddie Frith, Percy Goodman, M. D. Whitworth, Maurice Cann, Ernie Lyons, Jack Brett, Derek Farrant, Jock West, John Hartle, Derek Minter, Malcolm Uphill, Derek Ennett, Bob Anderson, Alastair King, Joe Potts, Dennis Parkinson, C. B. Bickell, Alan Shepherd, Noel Christmas, Reg Dearden, Doug Pirie, 'Griff' Jenkins, Dickie Dale, etc, etc. 'Lofty' England, a top Jaguar executive, was second on a Cotton-Python in the 1936 Lightweight Manx. In fact, of British road-racing 'greats', only John Surtees, Mike Hailwood and Stanley Woods haven't ridden in the 'Manx'.

44: *Rod Coleman at Horns Corner on the 1953 Senior TT 'Porcupine'.*

45: *Les Graham riding a 'Porcupine' in the 1950 Senior TT.*

46: *Bill Doran in the 1952 Swiss GP with the re-styled 'Porcupine'. The semi-streamlined head fairing carried the rev counter.*

47: *Rod Coleman on his 'Porcupine' at Mettet, Belgium, in 1952. Note enlarged rear suspension 'jam pots'.*

48: *The AJS works team in 1948. From left to right, Ted Frend, Les Graham and Jock West.*

49: *The beginnings of a great machine—Jock West testing a 7R 'Boys' Racer' in 1948 at what was then the Brands Hatch grass-track circuit. As soon as the machine was announced there was a lengthy waiting list.*

50: *Fergus Anderson regularly raced the 7R on the Continent. He is seen here at the Montjuich circuit, Barcelona, during a practice for the 1949 Spanish Grand Prix.*

51: *An artist's impression of the 1897 Mitchell-powered machine, which was the first complete motorcycle to be assembled by the Stevens family.*

52: *Rara avis: Joe Wright, at the start of an attempt on the world motorcycle speed record, with the ohc 1100 cc supercharged twin at Pendine in 1933. Behind are, left to right: R. R. Barber, Dickie Davies (Dunlops), 'Barry' Baragwanath, P. Brewster, Jock West, and a Lucas rep.*

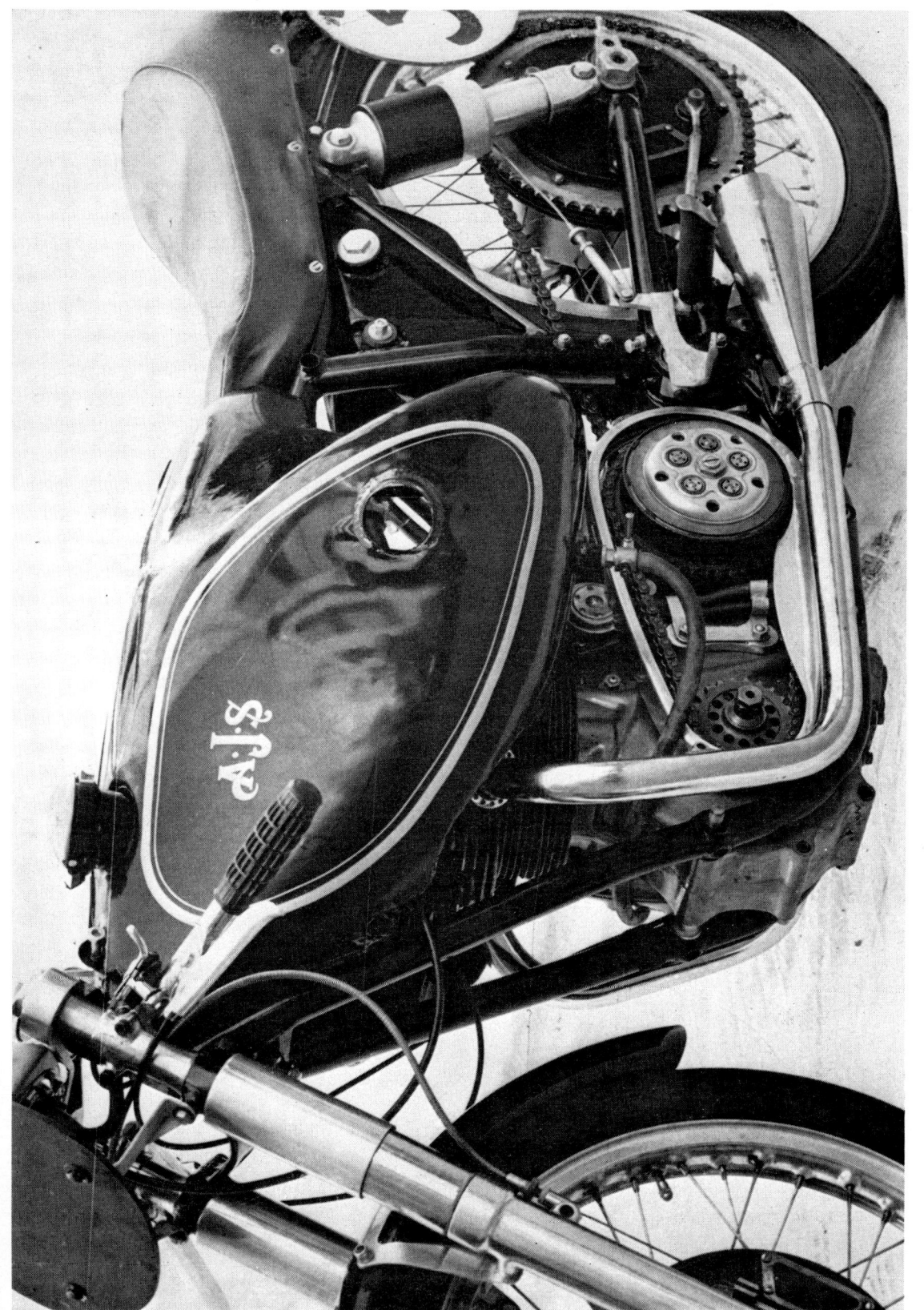

53: *Triple-knocker: close-up of Rod Coleman's 1954 Junior TT winner showing the streamlining effect as a result of the adoption of deep-section, pannier petrol tanks. This three-ohc machine also took world records at Montlhéry.*

54/55/56: *The 7R 'Boys' Racer' remained basically unchanged during its production life, apart from improvements to the power unit. However, subtle changes can be spotted. In 1960, for instance (centre) the petrol tank had lost its bulge and become more compact, while the rear brake operation was also changed. This was again modified for 1961 (bottom) and petrol was taken to the carburettor via the top of the float-chamber.*

57: *A line of partially assembled 7Rs in 1962 in the racing section at Plumstead—possibly one of the last batch to be completed. The massive backbone-type top tube and the double-loop frame can be clearly seen. The general design has much in common with the 1969 Y4 '250' frame.*

58: *Jack Williams (left), racing manager and chief development engineer, seen with Peter Murphy, also of AMC, and a 1962 7R. Williams was responsible for much of the success of the 'Boys' Racers' by greatly improving the output and reliability of the ohc engine.*

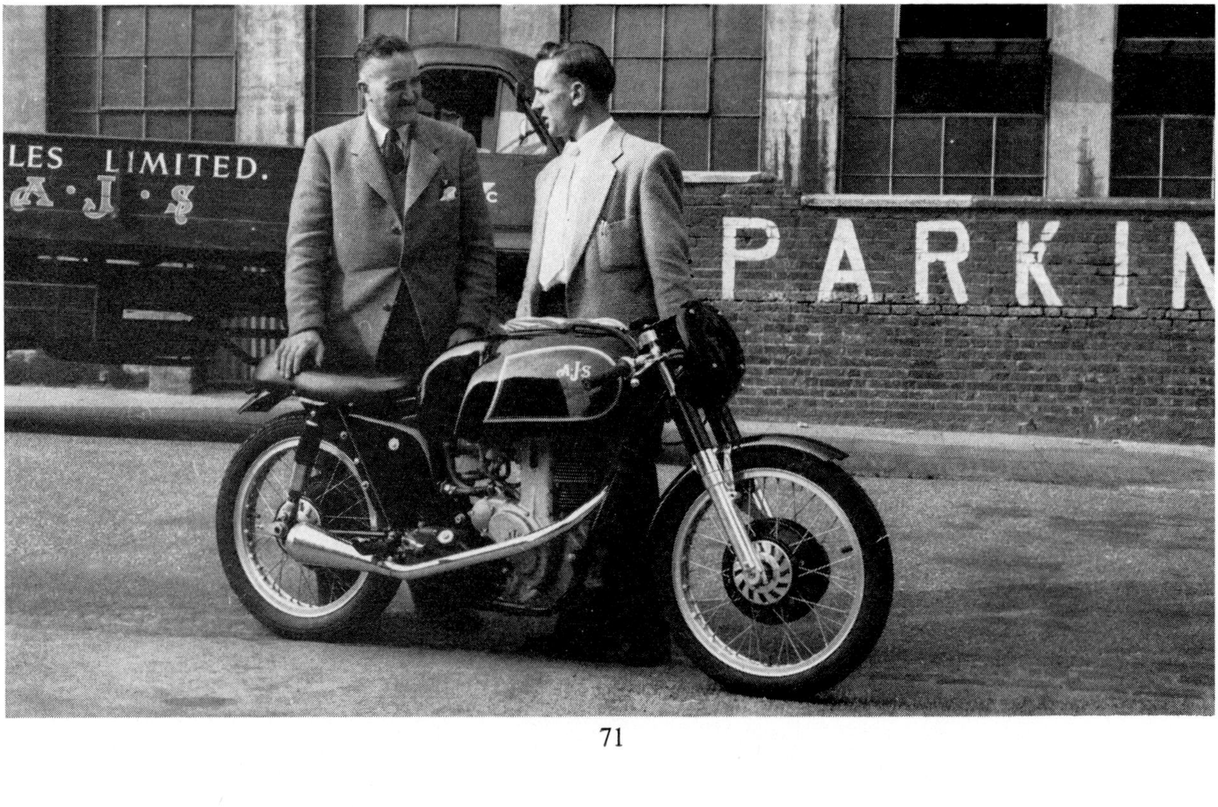

59: *Swedish rider Bill Nilsson installed a 7R engine into a frame, largely made up of bits and pieces from a 16C, and with outsize brake-drums. He was the first European Motocross Champion in 1957 on this machine. Using a 500 cc AJS, he won the first 500 cc World Championship in 1959.*

60: *The 1958 347 cc MCS 'Scrambler' was developed from the all-conquering 16C.*

Chapter 10

AJS production machines, 1911-1919

HAVING ESTABLISHED a profitable proprietary engine business, the Stevens brothers had for several years been thinking in terms of becoming motorcycle constructors in their own right. They had been building several components for other makers, including frames, and Jack and Joe Stevens had been competing regularly in trials and speed events on various machines fitted with Stevens engines. Most successful of the range of power-units was the side-valve of 292 cc (70 × 76 mm) which had been fitted in Wearwell, Woolf, Clyno and other machines.

During 1910, a prototype was built in the Screw Company's sheds and so encouraging were the results that Jack decided to enter the Junior TT with pre-production machines. As the name Stevens was associated with the proprietary engine side of the rapidly expanding business, as was related in an earlier chapter, the initials AJS were adopted and first appeared in the entry list for the Isle of Man races.

A new engine was developed for the race based on the 292 cc unit but altered to 70 × 77.5 mm, 298 cc, as the 1911 TT Junior regulations stipulated a maximum of 300 cc for a single-cylinder machine.

It was believed for many years that the TT machines ridden by Jack Stevens and his friend J. D. Corke were chain-driven but, in point of fact, they had belt-drive and a three-speed gearbox. It was late in 1911 that the first production AJS machines were marketed, the original pair bearing the registration numbers DA 607 and DA 608.

There were several changes from the 1911 TT machines. The side-valve engine had again been altered, this time to 74 × 81 mm, 348 cc. Although belt-drive was offered as an alternative in the original catalogue, there is no record of any production Ajays (as they soon became known) having other than all-chain drive. A two-speed counter-shaft-sliding gearbox or a three-speed unit was optional. In the latter case, the standard ratios were 12, 8 and 5 to 1. It was simply styled the 2¾ hp AJS and it was notable for the fact that the back wheel, clutch-sprocket, chains and kick-start mechanism could be removed without disturbing either primary or rear chain cases. A five-plate clutch with two cork-insert plates was used. Carburettor was by Amac and ignition by UH magneto. The wheels carried 26 × 2¼ inch tyres and the weight was given as 155 lb. The machine was priced at £53 11s.

The 'long-pattern' tanks were finished in white with a narrow blue panel broken in the centre to permit the inclusion of the new trade-mark, AJS. The belt-rim was retained for the rear brakes, the front being of the bicycle stirrup-pattern of the period. A simple diamond-type frame was used, the petrol tank being suspended from the single top-tube, and also serving to carry half a gallon of oil for the drip-feed oiling system.

'Sit-up-and-beg' handlebars were fitted and acetylene lighting could be provided as well as speedometer drive from the front wheel. For the more sporting rider, the 2¾ hp model could be supplied without rear chain covers, or with a kick-start and footrests in place of footboards. TT handlebars were also available.

Also at the 1912 Motorcycle Show was the first Vee-twin, the 6 hp Model D. This had the cylinders at 50 degrees, side valves, and each cylinder was of 74 × 81 mm, with a total capacity of 698 cc. The three-speed countershaft gearbox had ratios of 12.25, 7.5 and 4.75 to 1. Chains were totally enclosed, the wheels carried 650 × 75 mm tyres, carburettor was by Amac and magneto by UH. Finished in the same colours as the 2¾ hp model, the frame was fitted with sidecar lugs. In solo form it cost £72 9s.

By the time the 1913 Motorcycle Show came along, the Stevens brothers had found that many purchasers were having cylinder head gasket trouble, mainly due to removing the heads too frequently for valve-grinding and decarbonising, and being unable to obtain a proper seal again between head and cylinder barrel. Thus, in 1914, the Ajays had non-detachable heads and, on the Model B 2¾ hp model, the valves were enlarged to the same diameter as those on the twin. Also, the bore-stroke ratio was altered to 70 × 91 mm. All touring models from 1914 to 1916 had totally enclosed chains.

An external expanding rear brake was fitted to the twin but the 2¾ hp machine retained the dummy belt-rim-brake. The Model D appeared at the 1913 Show with a handsome, coach-built sidecar finished in black and gold and had been provided with extra-wide mudguards.

For 1915, appearance was altered by the adoption of dropped top-tube frames on all models and with forks having springs from the top of the links to the steering head. On the Model D, wheels were interchangeable.

A TT Sporting Special of the Model B was also marketed, with lightened piston, higher compression ratio, lightweight con rod, rear chain only partly shielded, and three sets of sprockets supplied. Jack Stevens reckoned that this machine was capable of 65 mph without any further tuning.

The non-detachable heads were continued until 1916 on all production models. In 1915, the four hp Model A 'all-purpose' twin of 65 × 85 mm (550 cc) supplemented the Model D, the engine size of which had been increased to 748 cc (74 × 87 mm). An Amac multiple-jet carburettor was fitted and ignition was by a Splitdorf EV magneto. Gear ratios were 16, 7.5 and 4.75 to 1. On the Model A, the ratios were 15, 9 and 5.75 to 1. Apart from engine size and gears, both twin-cylinder models were identical. Plain bearings were used throughout on the engines.

The period 1912-1914 was of great importance to the motorcycle industry. In 1912, a small offshoot of John Marston Ltd, makers of the Sunbeam, produced an overhead inlet valve engine, which was fitted to the Sun, which had no connection with Marstons. The engine was styled Villiers, after the name of the street in which the works were situated, which had in turn been named after a prominent Victorian statesman. The first production Sunbeams appeared with distinctive green and silver tanks and were notable for the superb quality of the engineering. A water-cooled, twin-cylinder, two-stroke Scott, with Frank Applebee in the saddle, won the Senior TT in 1912. A concern called Swan came out with a startling rotary 'four' with spring-frame by means of pivoting link.

The Burney brothers went into production as proprietary-engine makers, using a 499 cc unit with outsize flywheel located outside the crankcase, a feature usually found only on horizontally opposed twins and 'in-line fours'. This engine was based on a racing unit built in 1910 by de Havillands. The old-established Humber company evolved an ingenious, albeit unsuccessful, three-cylinder engine with the curious disposition of a single 370 cc cylinder in front and a pair of 185 cc ones at the rear, the latter offset for the two-way-throw crankshaft.

The Stevens brothers carefully studied these and other innovations but were convinced that the future of AJS lay in more orthodox machinery, with lightweight 'singles' for solo work and big-twin 'sloggers' for sidecar outfits. Undoubtedly they were influenced by the beautiful engineering of the Sunbeams, and in their own production machines sought to emulate the legendary immaculate finish of the Marston machines.

Whilst not denying for an instant that George Brough's splendid big-twin Brough Superiors of the 1920s and 1930s fully deserved the soubriquet 'The Rolls-Royce of Motorcycles', I believe that this could truthfully be said of the John Marston machines. The later 'beams, with their black and gold tanks, were finished to the most perfect standards of stove-enamelling which also applied to all non-bright parts. As for the latter, one method of obtaining the highly polished finish on aluminium and on nickel-plated copper exhaust pipes has seldom been equalled. By 1914, AJS machines were acknowledged as having a finish comparable to that found on far more expensive machinery, a tradition which has been maintained to this day.

AJS continued the production of the two types of machine until early 1916, when the resources of the new Graiseley House factory were given over to the production of precision components for the aircraft industry. Contracts for building machines for the Services had gone to Triumph, BSA, Clyno, Royal Enfield, P & M and Douglas.

Historian James Sheldon, in his excellent book *Vintage and Veteran Motorcycle* (published by Batsford), recounts how Sunbeams were given a contract for 50 machines for the Allies. Old John Marston almost had a fit when he discovered that the contract stipulated belt-drive. So if anyone ever discovers a belt-drive 3½ hp Sunbeam it would indeed be a rarity for, to the intense disgust of Marston, all 50 machines had to be converted from chain to belt before being despatched.

During the war years Jack Stevens and his brothers had plenty of opportunity to study the advances being made in the use of light alloys. They also came into contact with the designers and constructors of the various aero engine builders who, apart from the sleeve-valve addicts, maintained that maximum efficiency could only come from an overhead valve layout. As early as 1914, 'Pa' Norton had come to the same conclusion and had engaged a brilliant young engineer, Gilbert Smith, to work on an ohv unit, but this had to be shelved owing to the War.

Only the twin-cylinder 6 hp model was exhibited at the 1919 Motorcycle Show. The engine was of 748 cc (74 × 84 mm), but new detachable cylinder heads were fitted and both wheels were now detachable without the need to disturb the spindles. Stronger front forks had dual central springs. The wheels were now fitted with 700 × 80 mm tyres, electric lighting was optional and a luxurious sidecar with glass windscreen could also be obtained. A TB magneto was fitted, transmission was by a three-speed sliding-gearbox and, as in 1914, there was total enclosure of the chains. A few models were produced with 74 × 81 mm (698 cc) engines, presumably the makers using the con rods, pistons and heads of the 1913 pattern before the short-lived 'solid' cylinders were introduced. AJS finish was now standardised in black and gold.

The 2¾ hp model was listed at 47 guineas and there was a long, long waiting list. It was virtually unchanged from the 1915 machine except for the use of a TB magneto. Secondhand pre-war models were fetching exorbitant prices, often more than double the cost of a new machine. War gratuities were being lashed out in the purchase of anything on wheels and this no doubt led to the arrival of scores of cyclecars, many of which could best be described as 'rickety'.

George Poultney had developed the flywheel magneto for Villiers who, since 1914, had concentrated entirely on small-capacity two-stroke engines. By the beginning of 1920 the firm was supplying about 300 manufacturers, and had also cashed-in on the sudden, but short-lived, craze for motor-scooters.

During the latter part of 1919 the Stevens brothers had been doing a lot of experimenting and testing with an overhead valve unit in the 2¾ hp frame. The first complete machine was probably DA 4150, a prototype of a long line of successful ohv Ajays which were described in the chapter, 'The Big Port'.

Chapter 11

1920-1929

IT WAS NOT UNTIL the 1923 Motorcycle Show that the production ohv '350' was announced. Known as the Super Sports, it was the result of a stringent testing programme by the Stevens brothers. It was a logical development of the 'big port' but with certain modifications designed to ensure a long life of the working parts. Finish was really excellent and the little AJS looked every inch a thoroughbred.

Unlike the TT machine, splash-type lubrication was featured and the 5/18th inch big-end rollers were fixed by a pressed-in phosphor-bronze bush. A nickel-steel con rod was employed, with a hollow gudgeon pin for the four-ring aluminium-alloy piston. Standard ratios of the three-speed gearbox were 9.4, 6.1 and 5.0 to 1. The multi-plate clutch had cork inserts, and expanding brakes were provided front and rear. For competition purposes the combined rear mudguard and carrier was made quickly detachable. The machine could be supplied with a straight-through exhaust or tubular silencer. The sturdy frame was of the well-tried diamond pattern and the petrol tank, finished in black with gold lines and lettering, was carried between the two top tubes. The oil tank was located on the saddle tube.

AJS enterprise in going over to overhead valves for the 1920 TT had forced rivals to follow their example. For 1924, ohv models were listed by Norton, Rover, New Hudson, BSA, New Imperial, and by Cotton and Sheffield-Henderson with new outside-flywheel Blackburne engines. This engine was also fitted to Rex-Acme.

The best-selling $2\frac{3}{4}$ hp side-valve Model B was continued with few alterations, except for the adoption of a three-speed gearbox and internal-expanding brakes. Aluminium pistons were now employed on the big twin model, which had undergone several refinements, notably the provision for Lucas magdyno equipment and more generous mudguarding.

For 1925, the ohv Super Sports had the inlet port moved right to the rear of the cylinder head and TT-type tulip valves with $1\frac{5}{8}$ inch heads were fitted. However, unlike the TT engine, both valves were of the same diameter and the exhaust port was slightly reduced in size. The racing-pattern piston, with recesses for the valves, was adopted and the Amac carburettor replaced by a Binks

'mousetrap'. A Lucas magneto was standardised. Engine dimensions were unaltered, ie 74 x 81 mm (349 cc).

Changes to the 799 cc twin-cylinder machine included the substitution of a 'long' tank for the rather ungainly saddle pattern. The frame was, more or less, an elongated version of the '350', with the tank carried below the curved top-tube. The latest type of roller bearings were fitted to the big-ends. It had been planned to increase the capacity to over 900 cc but this was abandoned and dimensions remained as before, namely each cylinder was of 399.5 cc (74 × 93 mm).

For 1926, AJS produced the first ohv '500', an enlarged version of the Super Sports with a 498 cc (84 × 90 mm) engine. Both 350 cc and 500 cc engines had followed the TT units in having duralumin rockers, double-row rollers for the big-ends, plain bearings elsewhere, and 5.5 to 1 compression ratio. Lubrication to the rocker gear was by means of a rubber cover packed with graphited grease. Gear ratios on the larger-engined machine were 15, 8.3 and 4.6 to 1. The steel-strap method of securing the cylinder head was abandoned, two long bolts now leading to the crankcase.

All four models were virtually unchanged for 1927 but a new Model H9 side-valve was added to the range. It had the same dimensions as the ohv model, 84 × 90 mm (498 cc), and was intended as a dual-purpose machine, solo or sidecar.

The AJS range for 1928 was the most comprehensive yet presented by the rapidly expanding company. Three completely new models were added, 350 cc and 500 cc overhead camshaft machines, and a 248 cc (66 × 75 mm) side-valve—a sort of scaled-down version of the ever-popular '350'.

Described fully in the chapter 'The "cammy" AJS', the K7 and K10 production machines closely followed the 1927 TT entries. The engines had the chain-driven overhead camshaft with patented Weller tensioning device and additional friction damper. Dry-sump lubrication was featured, with a Pilgrim tandem pump. The crankshaft was supported in roller bearings with a double-row on the drive side. Caged rollers of the double-row pattern were used for the big-ends, and the compression ratio was 6.75 to 1.

Three-speed gearboxes were fitted with a hand-change, and ratios for the '350' were 10.31, 6.78 and 5.52 to 1. For the '500', they were 9.16, 5.64 and 4.65 to 1. In both cases, dimensions of the engines were identical to those of the ohv models. Prices were remarkably reasonable, being £62 for the '350', and £73 for the '500'.

AJS engineering was certainly progressive, but in the matter of styling somebody boobed. All Ajays had the old-fashioned 'long' tanks, whilst the majority of manufacturers had gone over to the 'new-look' saddle-tanks. This was all the more curious because AJS had started out with a saddle-tank on the original 1920 ohv model. Oddly enough Sunbeam, Triumph and Douglas were also caught napping with the old-style tanks between the frame top-tubes.

Nevertheless, even though the obsolescent frames and tanks were on the complete range, the Ajays were most attractive machines. Not all riders cared for the bulbous 'new look' but they were in the minority, and the four manufacturers all had to do a spot of quick thinking for 1929.

There followed hectic days in the drawing office at Graiseley House. Dozens of designs were made and scrapped until the Stevens brothers were satisfied. The result was a range of really beautiful machines with entirely new single-top frames, neat saddle tanks with purple panel, and centre-spring forks. The engines were cleaned up considerably, with enclosed push-rods and rockers for the ohv models and polished covers for the side-valves. To satisfy another popular demand, two-port heads were also made available. All models were referred to as 'M', thus the 350 cc and 500 cc ohc models became M7 and M10. The 'twin' was M1!

The double-port cylinder head had been pioneered by Triumph with their four-valve Ricardo engine and was, of course, featured on the four-valve Rudges. Certain two-stroke engines were so fitted, but why the arrangement suddenly appeared on two-valve engines was not quite clear. JAPs came out with a double-port unit which was installed in Howard Davies' HRD, the engine manufacturers reasoning that with this layout better volumetric efficiency was achieved. This may have been so, for Sunbeams followed suit with their very fast TT-winning Model '90', and also on the Model '80' 350 cc machine. New Hudson, Raleigh, Triumph and BSA also climbed on the two-port band-waggon. Twin exhaust pipes certainly provided a machine with a more balanced appearance, and on road models a better standard of exhaust silence resulted. Yet in the light of modern knowledge relating to cylinder head design, the majority of technicians agree that, with two-valve engines, a single-outlet exhaust pipe was equally efficient.

AJS also went over to the Webb-pattern front fork with large-diameter dampers and long central helical spring. The steering damper was incorporated in the head. Sunbeams were probably the last of the important manufacturers to retain the side-spring forks and, speaking from experience, a disconcerting speed-wobble was cured on a '90' by fitting Druids. Many manufacturers would like to have used the Castle type of forks, as fitted to Brough Superior, but this would have put prices up considerably, something that George Brough did not worry overmuch about on his expensive 'big twins'.

The AJS twin-cylinder machine had its engine capacity increased to 990 cc, still with side valves. Many people will agree that these AJS 'big twins' possessed hard-wearing qualities second to none. Flexibility was outstanding and for many years they had been regarded as the quietest machines on the market, both mechanically and in exhaust note.

Although the ohc Ajays had not been raced in the TT in 1928, considerable improvements had been made on both models. They now had new frames, centre-spring forks and a handsome saddle-tank which was slightly pistol-shaped. The braking system was modified, with both handlebar and foot operation for the front wheel.

Easily the best-seller in the AJS range was the single-port, ohv '350' which had been adding to its reputation with countless successes in trials.

Chapter 12

1930-1939

WITH 117 WORLD RECORDS to their credit during 1929 (See Chapter 15), A. J. Stevens and Co Ltd embarked on a most ambitious programme for 1930. Most of the machines used in record attempts had been prepared and tuned by Brooklands expert Nigel Spring, and many of the records stood to the credit of Bert Denly, one of Britain's foremost trackmen. Several of the features which had contributed to this unprecedented spate of record-smashing were incorporated in the new models.

The Wolverhampton factory had never been busier. When the 1930 Series 'R' range was announced there were completely new departures from established AJS practice. These were four brand-new 'slopers'—two 350 cc and two 500 cc models. Sloping engines were by no means new, having been featured years before by P and M, then taken up by Montgomery, Dunelt, Cotton, and latterly by BSA. It was the success of BSA that dictated the new fashion. AJS had been caught napping with their 1928 models, having retained the old diamond-type frame and 'long' petrol tank, but this time the machines were bang up to date.

The new frame for the AJS 'slopers' was of the semi-cradle variety, with duplex chain stays. The single top rail and down tube were of 1¾ inch diameter, the gauge of the steel used being heavier than on previous models. The rear down tube was carried below the bottom bracket forming the engine plates. The inclined engine enabled the magneto to be located behind the cylinder barrel and on the same platform were carried the gearbox and the battery. The front forks were re-designed with a longer central spring and slightly larger friction dampers. The steering damper had its arm fixing beneath the head. Brakes were enlarged and the anchorages in front were also attached to both fork blades, the operating cable being contained in one of the blades. The three-speed gearbox was entirely new and incorporated an enclosed kick-start mechanism. The gear change quadrant was located on the offside of the handsome black and gold saddle tank.

As for the overhead valve engines, the influence of racing and record-breaking was much in evidence. Double-row roller bearings were employed for the big-ends and were carried in duralumin cages, the two rows being separated by a thick oil film. The crankshaft ran on ball bearings, the drive side being double-row. The entire crank assembly had been stiffened up considerably, including the use of an enlarged crank pin. Port angles were altered, and a thicker cylinder head employed. The steel-tipped duralumin push-rods were fully enclosed. The rockers had throat springs added to eliminate valve gear rattle.

The heads were all of the two-port pattern, the exhausts being heavily plated, terminating in Brooklands-pattern silencers with fishtails. Special new assembly equipment had been installed at the factory to ensure accurate balancing of con rods, flywheels and pistons.

The side-valve engines had the same internal treatment but the traditional vertical finning on the head had been replaced by horizontal fins. Valve gear was neatly enclosed in a light-alloy cover. All models had dry-sump lubrication.

Thus the inclined engine models comprised side-valve and two-port ohv machines of 349 cc and 498 cc. A new two-port ohv '250' was also introduced, the engine being basically similar to the larger units. This engine, and a 349 cc side-valve unit, were vertically mounted in what were more or less the 1929 frames, stiffened at the rear somewhat. The range of road machines was completed by the 996 cc big-twin, which incorporated many of the improvements found on the other machines.

Apart from detail modifications, the 349 cc and 498 cc overhead camshaft machines (now R7 and R10) were virtually unchanged, but appearance was enhanced by the adoption of the black and gold finish of the other models. As a special concession, AJS were prepared to offer chromium or nickel plating on the production model tanks for £1 extra. Looking back, the prices of these machines were staggering to 1969 eyes. The '250' cost as little as £40 (less than $100 today), and the 'big twin' was only £63, plus £5 10s extra for full electric lighting.

Rumours that all was not well with the financial structure of A. J. Stevens and Co (1914) Ltd did not prevent the concern from announcing an even more ambitious programme for 1931. Sensational was an understatement when it came to the new 'Transverse Twin'. This was completely new throughout, powered by a 50 degrees, side-valve, twin-cylinder engine of 498 cc, mounted across the frame, the dimensions of each cylinder being 55 × 75 mm. The cylinder heads were of light alloy, each being secured to the crankcase by seven bolts. The valves were operated by separate cam-shafts, placed outside the Vee, inclined towards the cylinder axis. Both exhaust ports faced forward. A short driveshaft, provided with Hardy-Spicer flexible couplings, took the power to the four-speed gearbox and thence by chain to the rear wheel. The power-unit was installed in a neat frame which had duplex tubes for the front and rear sections.

Transverse twins had been tried before, notably by the P and M company with their ingenious Granville-Bradshaw designed 250 cc ohv Panthette in 1927, which was really never developed properly. This new AJS, however, had undergone a lengthy testing and development programme and from all accounts it performed extremely well, handled admirably, and had an even higher degree of silence than the 'big twin'.

So the complete programme for 1931 comprised four 'slopers', ie, side valves of 350 cc and 500 cc, and equivalent ohv models. Vertical - engine machines were a side-valve '350', the two-port '250' and the two camshaft models. To these were added the new transverse twin and an even more refined version of the 996 cc Vee-twin.

Early in 1931, although production of all models was continued, A. J. Stevens and Co Ltd went into liquidation. BSA tried to obtain control but in the middle of the year the entire motorcycle company, with all assets, was purchased by H. Collier and Son Ltd, and it was decided to move the production of AJS to Plumstead. The new owners refrained from exhibiting at the Motorcycle Show as there would be too much involvement in the change-over, both as regards personnel and machines.

After a brief period of production, the transverse twin was dropped. The ohc models also underwent the same fate, and neither types were listed for 1932. Improvements were made to the 'big twin' which had already been put in hand by the old company. These included 'squaring' the dimensions of the cylinders to 85.5 × 85.5 mm, the use of caged roller-bearing big-ends, seven-stud fixing for the aluminium cylinder heads, and the latest Amal carburettor. A new cradle frame was employed, capacity of the saddle-tank increased to 3½ gallons, and a four-speed gearbox of Sturmey-Archer origin installed. The Colliers, however, felt that the days of the big-twin sidecar outfit were numbered as, according to the sales charts, these were being replaced by 500 cc machines, and by 600 cc 'Big Four' singles.

Production of the 'cammy' Ajays was resumed in 1933, as is recounted in an earlier chapter, the chief change being a new cylinder head with horizontal finning. For 1934, the entire range was completely revised and the term 'big port' was used to describe three models of 250 cc, 350 cc and 500 cc, which bore a close affinity to Matchless machines. The first 'big port' had been announced during 1932, the 498 cc 33B 8. Completing the range were two-port 350 cc and 500 cc machines, a couple of single-cylinder side-valves of 350 cc and 500 cc, whilst the 996 cc big twin was retained. Ribbed chromidium brake drums were featured. The 350 cc 'big port' had a Burman gearbox, as used successfully by George Rowley in trials.

The overhead camshaft machines were made in two forms, racing and trials, the latter being styled the Trophy model, probably to cash in on Rowley's success in the 1932 ISDT. Rowley himself favoured the ohv 350 cc 'big port' as a trials machine and it seems likely that very few of the Trophy machines were actually built and sold.

It was at the 1935 Motorcycle Show at Olympia that the four-ohc 'four' was exhibited. Despite the tremendous interest created and the attractive low price, it was never put into production. The 'four', and the racing versions, are described elsewhere.

The 'Trophy' model was quietly dropped, only the racing 'cammies' being listed for 1935. No more 'big twins' were produced. Meanwhile the technicians had been busy. Weight-saving was the main consideration, for the 1934 machines were all considered to be too heavy. So more use was made of electron and light-alloy materials, and a result of this was that the weight of the ohv TT '350' was brought down to the highly satisfactory figure of 260 lb.

Lessons from the TT were incorporated in the 'cammy' models. Close-ratio Burman gearboxes with a new type of positive foot change were employed, additional check-springs fitted to the front forks, the magneto re-located on a more rigid and sloped platform, larger petrol tanks fabricated, and hairpin valve-springs used. There was virtually a no-change policy for 1936, the range being retained *in toto*.

For 1937, racing policy was advanced a stage further when Colliers indicated that after the TT absolute replicas of the 350 cc ohc machines would be marketed at the attractive price of £87 5s. These would have the new double-loop frame with single down tube and megaphone exhaust system. Each machine would be individually tested at Brooklands before delivery.

Although a spring-frame 'cammy' made its appearance in the 1938 TT, the replicas produced up until the outbreak of the Second World War all had the 1937 frames. It was in 1938 that the term 7R was first used; the ohc machines had been described by various type-numbers, including R7, R12 and R15, the 'R' merely denoting racing. The TT spring-frame consisted of short pivoted arms, to which were attached spring boxes, supported top and bottom by the main frame. It was the intention to adopt this type of spring-frame for most of the range but, with first Munich, and then the outbreak of war, all programmes had to be shelved. The Plumstead factory was given over mainly to the production of Matchlesses for the Services and, up to 1940, a few Ajays. It was during the War that the 'Teledraulic' front forks were pioneered, with such great success that, when production was resumed after the cessation of hostilities, it replaced the older girder pattern on both AJS and Matchless machines.

Chapter 13

1946-1959

AFTER THE WAR, AJS production was further streamlined by AMC in line with the Matchless range. The Vee-twin had been dropped and one could say that, apart from the finish and name on the tank, Matchless and AJS machines were barely distinguishable as regards mechanical specification. However, the decision to race the 'Porcupine' showed clearly that every attempt was going to be made to keep the famous initials going. Also, as a further aid to sales, AMC formed a competitions department under George Rowley which had a most efficient staff and, eventually, brilliant riders.

So successful was the AJS trials exercise that, in 1948, competition versions of the standard 350 cc 16M and the Model 18 '500' were marketed. These were the 347 cc (69 × 93 mm) and the 498 cc (82.5 × 93 mm) models, priced at £148 11s 10d and £161 5s 10d. The frames were modified to provide shorter wheelbases and a larger ground-clearance was provided. Transmission was by Burman four-speed gearbox and both engines were of the single-port type, with enclosed overhead valves and rockers. Outwardly the only difference from the standard Matchless engines was that the magneto was located in front of the cylinder. The standard 16M was priced at £142 4s 10d and the bigger 18 at £154 18s 10d. All four prices included purchase tax. These machines formed the basic output from AJS for several years.

The only 'real' AJS was the 7R, with its chain-driven overhead camshaft engine, which appeared in the 1947 TT and was available in production form in 1949. Although described in a separate chapter, it is worth noting that the '350' would attain 100 mph, with a 5.14 to 1 final drive ratio, using a 21-tooth engine sprocket and a 54-tooth rear sprocket. Like the ohv models, Teledraulic front forks were used and the frame was a development of the 1939 TT pattern with swinging-link rear suspension.

New frames were devised for 1949, cylinder heads redesigned, and all ohv AJS engines provided with hairpin-type valve-springs. Magnetos were still located in front of the cylinders. As on the 'Boys' Racer', KE 965 steel-alloy valves were used for the competition machines. It was in that year that Matchless brought out the G9 vertical twin, later to be installed in AJS machines as well.

Continued success in trials, and with the road-racing 7Rs, maintained a steady demand for Ajays in the 1950s. There was still plenty of advanced thinking in the development and experimental section but AMC's standardisation programme made it unlikely that anything new would be produced unless a really good market could be guaranteed. The AJS designers came up with a highly successful 'triple-knocker' engine for the 7R but, despite Rod Coleman's win in the 1954 Junior TT, the Ike Hatch-designed power-unit was considered by the AMC directors to be too expensive to produce for what they envisaged would be a limited market.

In 1955 the development section again produced a three-ohc engine but this would have been even more costly to produce, requiring special gears for the drive. With the appointment of Jack Williams as Chief Development Engineer it was thought that AMC would go ahead with a production version of the 7R3, but in 1955 his talents were switched over to concentrate on the 'Boys' Racer'. Under the aegis of Williams, the 7R was improved considerably, although production was comparatively small owing to the hand-built methods used in the assembly and construction of each machine.

Without a doubt it was the refined quality of these 7Rs which made them so popular with riders. In events such as the Manx Grand Prix, the 'Boys' Racers' predominated. For instance, in the 1955 Junior event there were no less than 39 'Boys' Racers', of which 28 finished.

The high standard of AJS engineering was due to the complete re-tooling of the Plumstead factory, starting in 1953. As AMC also produced Norton, James and Francis-Barnett machines, the directors were convinced that even more standardisation was required to ensure a useful return. It was decided to increase production of four-stroke engines, design and produce a two-stroke for James and Francis-Barnett to replace the proprietary unit, and also to manufacture all gearboxes needed for the entire AMC range. This cost around a million pounds from 1953-1958, and the Herbert Organisation of Coventry were consultants, a great deal of the new equipment being made and supplied by Alfred Herbert Ltd.

By 1958 over 400 engines and 650 gearboxes per annum were being produced at Plumstead. In addition, AJS and Matchless were assembled at the Woolwich factory, Norton and James in Birmingham, and Francis-Barnett in Coventry.

Yet, no matter how efficient the machine tools, the Plumstead works was totally unsuited to planned and economical production. They were badly sited in a district infamous for traffic density, various sections were spread all over the place, and there was always a tremendous demand for more space. It is all to the credit of the workers that such splendid machines were turned out—probably because tradition died hard. AJS technicians, in particular, were immensely proud of their handiwork.

1958 saw many changes in a nine-model range, all, of course, being complementary to Matchless, apart from the 7R racing model. The ohv 350 cc models were the 16MS, the 16MC (trials) and the 16MCS (scrambler). As regards the 500 cc singles, there were the 18S and the scrambler edition, the 18CS. The vertical twins were the 492 cc 20, the 592 cc 30, and the 30CS scrambler version.

Lucas alternators replaced the generators and magnetos of the earlier single-cylinder models which now had coil ignition. The 'twins' retained magnetos but had DC generators. The pressed-steel chaincase of 1957 was replaced by a new cast-aluminium unit, which was also used to provide a rigid mounting for the stator of the camshaft-driven alternator.

A 30CS Sportstwin was also listed, with a specially tuned 592 cc engine, having siamesed ports and a compression ratio of 8.5 to 1. With purchase tax, this cost £299 8s. The 7R, fully pre-pared to FIM road-racing regulations, was listed at £417 18s 3d, with purchase tax.

In 1959, AJS adopted what was known as the 'blue look' on the petrol tanks, with the option of two-tone (blue/grey), black with chromium centre, or the classic black and gold. Earlier a brand-new '250' had been introduced and had already become so popular that this Model 14 was extended with the 14CS, a special motocross machine. This was the first new AJS motorcycle to be specifically designated for motocross work, although the existing scrambler versions of the Models 16 and 18 had been adapted for motocross by several riders and could now be obtained as such from the factory.

The requirements of American and Canadian customers were met with a new version of the Model 31CS, 600 cc vertical twin, ideal for the long-distance desert races that had become so popular on that side of the Atlantic Ocean. Basically, this was also the twin-cylinder motocross model.

The '250' had a bore and stroke of 70 mm and 65 mm (248 cc), but otherwise closely followed the existing 350 cc and 500 cc 'singles', even to the extent of duralumin rockers, steel-tipped 'dural' push-rods and hairpin valve springs. Normal compression ratio was 7.8 to 1, but on the competition model this was raised to 10 to 1. With light-alloy mudguards, it weighed about 300 lb, almost the same as the famed 16MC.

Chapter 14

1960-1968

FOR 1960, THE MOTOCROSS version of the '350' was dropped but a new lightweight, described as the Light 350 or Model 8, was introduced, based on the 250 cc model. The entire range had been re-designed, with full duplex frames, which were also to be found on the 500 cc Scrambler and the Speedtwin. Continuing the application of racing experience to production machines, all engines again had port diameters increased, with a con-sequent step-up in power-outputs. The 31CSR Speedtwin was becoming a popular mount for pro-duction machine racing, scoring many victories at events up and down the country, as well as in the USA.

With its wonderful record in 'Six Days' events, the 347 cc 16MC was acknowledged as being *the* machine for trials. A total of 14 models was the largest ever offered under the name of AJS but, of course, with the exception of the 7R, these were also the basic Matchless machines.

The range was continued for 1961 with little alterations, these mainly concerning the 14CS '250' which had the crankshaft stiffened up with the addition of a larger-diameter crankpin, and revised ignition. The compression ratio was upped to 10.5 to 1. There was again a 'no-change' policy for 1962, but AMC decided to cut the range of AJS models considerably and call a halt to the produc-tion of the 7R. It was stated that the costs of con-structing this more or less hand-built machine could no longer be economical and that the price which would have to be asked made it far too expensive a proposition.

The 'Boys' Racer' had had a great run, the AMC edition having been in continuous produc-tion for 14 years. It was still very much a power to reckon with and during 1962 many racing suc-cesses had been achieved at home and abroad by riders such as Gary Hocking, Hughie Anderson, Phil Read, Alan Shepherd, Mike Duff, Alastair King and W. (The Pretzel) Wetzel. The passing of the 'Boys' Racer' marked yet another milestone in the history of AJS and there were glum faces at Plumstead when the news was announced.

This left the twin-cylinder 31CSR as the sole AJS which could be used for racing and, from 1963 onwards, AJS and Matchless products were practically identical, differences only being ap-parent on machines specially prepared for com-petitions, such as the 16MC, which still had the magneto mounted in front of the cylinder.

For 1963 the various models had sprouted exotic names which were disregarded by died-in-the-wool Ajay enthusiasts. This must have been communicated to the publicity people at Plum-stead, for the type numbers were carefully re-tained. Thus we had the Model 14 Sapphire, the 14CSR Sapphire Supersports, 16 the Sceptre, the 18 Statesman, the 31 Swift, and the 31CSR Hurricane. The 16MC became the Experts, and the 18CS the Southerner. The range had been reduced to eight models and several gay colour schemes were avail-able. More power was given to the 31CSR by raising the compression ratio to 10.25 to 1 and by the provision of twin Amal carburettors.

In the following years the production of AJS and associated machines began to fall off. With bigger pay packets, young men tended to invest in small cars, leaving motorcycling to dedicated groups of people, or to the riders of ultra-small-capacity machines who used their mounts as trans-port to and from their places of employment. Yet, in the USA, the sport of motorcycling was boom-ing, especially in California, where there was an ever-increasing demand for large, powerful machines.

AJS reluctantly abandoned competitions in 1965, although the 16C and 18C models continued to be produced in relatively small numbers. The trials team of Mick Andrews, the two Gordons, McLaughlin and Blakeney was transferred to another AMC section, James. Then the old AMC concern was absorbed in the new Norton Villiers combine. First things first, and Norton were the initial make to receive a face-lift — and what a face-lift! The modern Norton Commando, with its 750 cc twin-cylinder engine and complete freedom from vibration, is one of the world's finest motor-cycles.

The Chairman, Dennis Poore, had made up his mind that AJS would, in the future, rise to even greater heights than those envisaged by the Stevens brothers over 60 years ago. A return to competi-tions was the obvious thing to do and, like Jack Stevens and his brothers so many years ago, Norton Villiers have come out with a single-cylinder machine — the two-stroke Y4, 250 cc Scrambler. The story of the Y4 is told in the chapters 'AJS Revived' and '1969—and all that'.

We have now arrived at the year 1969. It may be nostalgic to harp on about the 'old days' but, looking back over six decades or so, it cannot be denied that the AJS contribution to motorcycling has been considerable. It should also be pointed out that the three leading makes in the Norton Villiers empire all sprang from rider-manufacturers of Edwardian days, namely Jack Stevens (AJS), Harry and Charlie Collier (Matchless) and John L. ('Pa') Norton (Norton). All four rode in the Isle of Man TT races as part of the development stage of their machines. Harry's brother Charlie won the 1907 'Single-cylinder' TT on a Matchless, and Harry himself won the all-comers event in 1909. Charlie's Matchless had an overhead-valve JAP engine and the winner of the 'twin' race was H. Rem Fowler on a Peugeot-powered Norton. Harry's Matchless had a twin-cylinder JAP engine. AJS did not, of course, enter the fray until 1911.

Yes indeed, when one ponders on those far-off days, it is difficult to understand why British manufacturers, who led the world for so many years, allowed themselves to become complacent regarding the threat from overseas. The Tourist Trophy races have been so much bound up with the development of the motorcycle that it is interesting to note that, since O. C. Godfrey won the 1911 Senior on an American Indian, not a single foreign-built machine won a TT until 1935, when Stanley Woods carried off both the Lightweight and the Senior on Italian Guzzis.

AJS fully realised the implications of that Senior Guzzi victory and, if only others had taken up the challenge which AJS offered with the 'fours' and later the 'Porcupines', then the future of the industry in Great Britain might have been completely altered.

The marque AJS has given so much to the motorcycle industry and it is hoped that Norton Villiers will have every possible success with the fascinating little Y4, particularly in the export markets where motocross machines could be really big business.

Chapter 15

record-breaking

DESPITE THE SCORES of world records held at one time or another by AJS, the Stevens brothers were never fully convinced that these had any direct influence on sales. In fact, they were interested only in one record—the fastest motorcycle on land. To that purpose, in 1929 they constructed a very special 1,100 cc Vee-twin with engine designed by Ike Hatch. This was, in effect, a double 'cammy', the cylinders being mounted on a common crankcase. This massive Vee-twin unit was mounted in an elongated version of the TT frame, the 500 cc barrels each bored out to give a swept volume of 548 cc (totalling 1,096 cc).

It looked a most workmanlike machine and, being designed to travel in a straight line, was not notable for either comfort or roadholding. Captain Owen Baldwin took it to Arpajon, but the highest recorded speed was around 121 mph and it seemed that as a land speed record-contender it was something of a flop. When the move was made to Plumstead, the big twin was inherited by the Colliers, and for many months lay forgotten in a corner of the development shops. Then, in 1933, interest was revived and the big twin was worked on again. Percy Brewster supplied a Zoller supercharger and several runs were made at Brooklands in preparation for the attempts.

Jock West states that it was a brute to handle and that a pair of Druid forks might have made a lot of difference. Factory rider Reg Barber, who took over after Jock had turned in several extremely rapid laps, went into a series of wobbles and came off on to the hard Brooklands concrete, almost at West's feet. Jock recalls feeding Barber with wild blackberries whilst awaiting an ambulance and a doctor to tend the unfortunate rider's broken collar bone.

A Mr Plaister, who had been concerned in Mobiloil's backing of the Lindbergh solo Atlantic flight, persuaded the oil company to back the AJS project. Journalist Laurie Cade was also concerned. Following unsuccessful attempts in Hungary, the big Ajay was taken to Southport for ex-Zenith record-holder Joe Wright to have a go on the famous sands. The record stood at 152 mph to the credit of Ernst Henne on a supercharged 500 cc BMW. Wearing his famous streamlined crash helmet, Wright made several runs up and down the measured distance. The best speed recorded in

one direction was 145 mph, with a mean average of 132 mph.

Thereafter the big Ajay twin lay forgotten for many years until, in 1965, it suddenly turned up in Tasmania, having arrived there from Australia. From all accounts it was in a pretty sorry state, with various parts missing, including the supercharger. Although it never held a record, it must be something of a collector's piece and it is hoped that an effort will be made to restore it to something approaching its original condition.

Record-breaking in general did not particularly interest the manufacturers and almost invariably attempts were made under the auspices of outside concerns, in some cases finance being provided by an oil concern. Nevertheless, the system of various oil companies and components makers paying bonuses according to results made it quite a profitable business for Brooklands tuners and those who supported their own racing stables. In the old Brooklands days there were several such establishments, with entrants, tuners and riders such as Nigel Spring, D. R. (Wizard) O'Donovan, E. C. 'Barry' Baragwanath, Bill Lacey, Doug Marchant, Vic Horsman, Chris Staniland, Eric Fernihough, J. S. Worters, Les Archer, Joe Wright, Bert Denly and many others.

In those days there was a certain amount of gamesmanship in record-breaking and riders who put up figures too high were not always popular with others in the 'circus'. One could have a fairly profitable year having one's speeds raised fractionally each time. The bonus-payers were happy enough, for each new record meant that there was all the more to advertise.

The FIM has always had a more reasonable attitude to records than its car counterpart, the FIA. The latter organisation insists that world records are those achieved over set distances and within set periods by the fastest cars, irrespective of capacity. All other records are merely described as International class records. The FIM acknowledges world records as being the fastest in each class. Thus, in the record books, motorcycles are credited with innumerable world records, whilst the majority of car figures are listed as International Class records.

To recount all the records which fell to AJS would take many pages, but it is worth recalling that, in 1929 at Montlhéry, Bert Denly put 104.51 miles into the hour and covered the flying kilometre at 107.02 mph. He was on Nigel Spring's ohc '500' which was normally used for Brooklands events. With the same machine and sidecar he did the flying kilometre at 96.71 mph—the fastest-ever for machines of up to 600 cc. It is also worth noting that his one-hour figures were better than those existing in both 750 cc and 1,000 cc classes. Partnered by C. R. Hough, he covered the 1,000 kilometres on the same machine at 86.34 mph. The pair also secured many other records with a '350'. The following year, Denly, on the same machine, sped over the flying kilometre at Arpajon at 118.98 mph—and that was 39 years ago !

When the FIM published the official list of world records achieved during 1929, no less than 117 of them were held by either Denly or Hough on AJS machines. I should think that this is a record by itself and may never be emulated.

The 'Porcupine' also did its share of record-breaking. At Montlhéry in 1948, Jock West, Les Graham and Georges Monneret took no less than 18 world records from two to six hours. West actually did a one-hour stint without goggles. He had acquired a new tinted pair but they didn't fit properly and, travelling at about 120 mph on the banking, they simply disappeared. To stop might have jeopardised the attempts, so Jock carried on gallantly.

Montlhéry was a popular venue for record-breaking and after 1928 practically every new record was accomplished on the French 'saucer'. Brooklands insisted on large-sized silencers and fish-tails but at Montlhéry open exhausts were permitted, and consequently much higher speeds could be obtained.

Chapter 16

AJS revived

DENNIS POORE was the driving force behind the new Norton Villiers Co which was created when his important Manganese Bronze concern acquired the assets of AMC. He realised that, in so far as future production of Norton, AJS and Matchless machines was concerned, there had to be some serious re-thinking. Complete reorganisation was essential, otherwise the manufacture of motor-cycles would not be an economic proposition.

Although the decision to move to a new factory at Andover, Hants, was taken in 1966, it was not until 1968 that full planning permission was obtained. The company's intention was to have this new factory in full operation by the middle of 1969. The site was ideal, presenting no difficulties in communications between Norton Villiers, outside suppliers and the company's other engineering resources. With the appearance of the modern Norton Commando '750', it was obvious that Norton Villiers Ltd had its finger on the pulse of current requirements. What to do as regards AJS was another story!

Poore himself had been prominent in motor racing during the immediate post-war period and had won the RAC Hill-Climb Championship with his 3.8-litre supercharged Alfa Romeo. He had also driven an MG and a Veritas (a sort of modified Type 328 BMW) with success, and had been a member of David Brown's works Aston Martin team and the Connaught Grand Prix team.

With Peter Walker as co-driver, he won the Goodwood 'Nine Hours' for Aston Martin in 1955. In the 1953 RAC British Grand Prix at Silverstone he took fourth place in a Connaught and would undoubtedly have finished much higher but for an unfortunate error in the pits, when he was given a bottle supposed to contain lemonade but which contained a large proportion of methanol!

Anyway, here was a chairman with an extensive background of competitions, together with engineering knowledge of a high order. With Norton plans already formulated, he had given a great deal of thought to the future of AJS and, in 1966, the opportunity to do something about it was presented by Peter Inchley. Riding a 'Villiers Starmaker Special', Inchley finished third in the Lightweight TT behind the works Hondas of Mike Hailwood and Stuart Graham. No British-built '250' had been in the first three since 1950, and none had come anywhere near lapping at the speeds which Peter Inchley accomplished. He averaged 91.43 mph for the 264 miles distance. Inchley's machine had a Villiers engine fitted into what was basically a Bultaco frame, and with six-speed transmission.

The designer-rider was an acknowledged two-stroke expert. Born in Smethwick, he had joined BSA in 1960 and, in the same year, started racing on his friend Stan Cooper's Ariel Arrow. He later went to Ariels, where he was concerned with much of the development work on that well-made two-stroke. His next move was to EMC, where he worked with Joe (The Professor) Ehrlich on two-strokes. He also rode for EMC in races and finished fourth in the 250 cc Spanish Grand Prix. Inchley joined the Villiers concern late in 1963.

So Norton Villiers decided that the name AJS would be applied to a 250 cc two-stroke and that the board of directors would back Peter Inchley in the 1967 Lightweight TT. Ken Sprayson, of Reynolds tubes, was commissioned by NV to construct the frame. This was of the backbone type, built up from $2\frac{1}{8}$ inch $\times$ 18 gauge steel tubing. Dual loops of $\frac{3}{4}$ inch diameter tubing ran from the steering head to act as front down-members, then passed under the engine to terminate on mountings for the rear damper assembly. A new AJS engine was planned and it was decided to retain the six-speed transmission for the TT.

However, the new engine could not be made ready in time and Inchley reverted to the 1966 unit, with which he had won races at Mallory Park and at Snetterton, as well as setting up a new 250 cc Brands Hatch record.

The AJS proved to be even faster in the Isle of Man than the Bultaco-based version, Inchley averaging 92.89 mph when he was forced to retire when placed fifth, owing to a serious error by the oil company concerned. When Inchley stopped to refuel, instead of the 'petroil' mixture, the tank was filled with neat fuel. A complete engine seizure was the result!

Nevertheless, there was little doubt that the AJS single-cylinder was as far advanced as any of the equivalent continental two-strokes. Inchley himself had been getting as much as 35 bhp at 8,500 rpm—and over 140 bhp per litre is a real achievement with a 'valveless' single-cylinder engine.

Racing in the TT was merely a means to an end, for the shrewd Dennis Poore saw immense opportunities for a 'scrambler' machine designed specifically for the booming sport of motocross. In late 1967, a prototype scrambler, the Y4 AJS, was completed and ridden for the first time in an important event by a brilliant young rider from Stroud, Andy Roberton, who had competed during 1966 on a CZ.

Then another young man, a rider-agent from Gloucester, was employed and entered for the opening round of the BBC Grandstand Trophy. His name was Malcolm Davis, and, at Canada Heights on Armistice Day 1967, he collected two points for a sixth place in the 250 cc section. At Kirkcaldy, Scotland, he added two more points for a third place. The final round was at Caerlon, comprising two separate events. Davis won the first one and was fourth in the second. His total of 19 points was exceeded only by World Motocross Champion Jeff Smith. He also gained three fourth places in rounds counting towards the ITV World of Sport Solo Championship.

The 1968 British Motocross Championships proved that AJS had arrived with a vengeance in the world of cross-country racing, for Malcolm Davis won the 250 cc title, competing against powerful opposition in the shape of works riders of Bultaco, CZ, Husqvarna and Greeves machines.

His path to the championship makes interesting reading. The opening round was the Cumberland Grand National, and Davis won the first event with Dick Clayton second on another AJS. At Glastonbury, Clayton was runner-up in the first heat with Davis likewise in the second. At this stage, the championship placings were as follows:

1 Derek Rickman (Bultaco) 26 points
2 Andy Roberton (Husqvarna) 18 points
3 Malcolm Davis (AJS) 16 points
4 Dick Clayton (AJS) 13 points
5 Arthur Browning (Greeves) 7 points
6 Fred Mayes (Montesa) 7 points

Round three was at Cleveland, Yorks, and the experienced Chris Horsfield replaced Derek Clayton in the AJS team for the Grand National. The reputation of the marque received a further shot in the arm when Horsfield won the first heat, overtaking race-leader Davis on the 11th lap. The latter finished fourth, slowing with electrical bothers.

Horsfield went like the wind in heat two, chased by three riders including Davis. Malcolm dropped back many places after ramming a tree and then Horsfield retired when his petrol tank came adrift. Davis plugged on, finally to take third place. Rickman did not compete at this meeting but still retained his 26 points, with Davis now only five points behind.

In round four, the Lancashire Grand National at Cuerden Park, Preston, Malcolm Davis really came into his own. The electrical bothers he had experienced in earlier events had now been eradicated. In the first heat, he won from Arthur Browning (Greeves) by almost half a minute. Davis also won heat two, with Browning again second.

This result put Davis and his AJS in an almost unassailable position, for there was only one round to go—at Nantwich, Cheshire. He had 37 points to the 26 of Rickman, the 23 of Roberton, and the 21 of Browning. Davis required just six points from the two heats to win the title. Rickman, who had been on the injured list with a damaged thumb, was fighting fit for the finals.

Alan Clough (Husqvarna), the 1967 British Champion, rode brilliantly in heavy rain on his home circuit to win, chased all the way by Rickman and Roberton. Davis fell off in the mud, remounted and fought back to third place. The title was his. His four points gave him 41, compared to Rickman's 32, the latter having finished second. Another third place in heat two merely increased his total to 45 points—nine more than Rickman.

This was indeed heartening to Norton Villiers— a Championship in what was virtually the first competition year of the new Y4. It was decided to enter Davis in the World Motocross Championships but, in these, he did not have the best of luck. On at least two occasions he was well out in front when in one event a plug lead came adrift and in another a contact-breaker spring broke. He did, however, manage to take fourth place in the Belgian Grand Prix and achieved the same placing in the Luxembourg Grand Prix. In the final table it was noteworthy that, in a list of placings dominated by Husqvarna, Bultaco and CZ machines, Malcolm's AJS was the highest-placed British entry.

For 1969, Peter Inchley was determined to organise an even stronger onslaught on motocross, national and international. Everyone agreed that the Y4 AJS was a pretty fair tool and that it could be a major export commodity to all countries where cross-country motorcycling sport was practised. In February, the first AJS scrambler was exported to Sweden. Inchley also attempted to sign up the Swedish star Olie Petersen, in the face

61: *The ohv 498 cc 18S of 1958 was a popular fast-tourer, as well as being an effective sidecar machine.*

62: *The machine that made the name AJS famous in trials throughout the world—the 347 cc 16C as it appeared in 1961.*

63: *A classic photograph: Peter Howdle's famous picture of Gordon Jackson on his 16C losing his one and only penalty point for a 'dab' on Grey Mare's Ridge when he scored his fourth win in the Scottish Six Days Trial.*

64: *The 'Jackson Dab' is perpetuated in the Edinburgh St George MC's club-rooms, along with the 'Spirit of the Scottish'. Seen here are 'Scottish' personalities Tommy Melville and Arthur MacNaughton.*

65: *A quartet of Y4s at Thruxton track at Andover, where part of the new works is to be located, with Andy Roberton (second from right) and members of the AJS competitions staff.*

66: *Forerunner of the Y4: Peter Inchley on his 247 cc two-stroke Villiers Starmaker Special at Parliament Square, Ramsey, when he finished third in the 1966 Lightweight TT.*

67: *Formidable trio: From left to right, Bob Manns, Hugh Viney and Gordon Jackson, who scored a hat-trick on their 16Cs by winning the manufacturers' award for AJS in the 1953, 1954 and 1955 Scottish Six Days Trials. Between them, Viney and Jackson had eight victories and the former had an individual hat-trick in 1947, 1948 and 1949.*

68: *Two Gordons, namely Blakeley (left) and McLaughlin, checking up a 16C before the start of the 1964 'Scottish'.*

69: *Malcolm Davis (right) on the Y4 AJS during a BBC TV event at Naish Hill in 1968. This was the same year that Davis won the 250 cc British Motocross Championship.*

70: *AJS riders Malcolm Davis and Andy Roberton (below) being briefed by SAS officers on details of the commando course they did in February 1969, in preparation for the World Motocross Championships.*

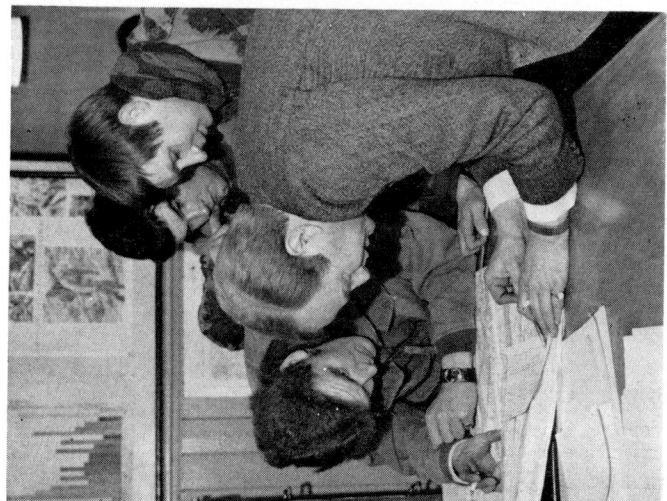

71: *Andy Roberton (Y4 AJS) defying all the laws of gravity during an early season scramble in 1969.*

72: *The remarkably rapid 250 cc Starmaker AJS TT machine—forerunner of the Y4 'Scrambler'.*

73: *The 1969 production AJS Y4 'Scrambler', the 250 cc two-stroke engine of which gives nearly 30 bhp, with good torque.*

74: *For the trials rider, the high ground-clearance 37A-T '250' is notable for its excellent handling and ideal torque characteristics.*

of fierce competition from Husqvarna and Suzuki; Olie, however, accepted the Japanese offer.

That splendid rider Andy Roberton joined Davis. AJS had adopted a most serious attitude towards competitions, so much so that both Davis and Roberton were sent to Wales on a special Commando course to toughen them up for the coming World Championship series. The course was specially evolved by the officers of Special Air Service for the AJS riders.

AJS had anything but good fortune in the World Championships. Davis set fastest lap in the Spanish GP and was building up a considerable lead of around ten seconds when water entered the engine. The same thing happened in the second leg when he was in second place. Roberton took five points for a sixth place.

In the Swiss GP, Davis was eliminated with a cracked plug in heat one and by a chain jumping the sprocket in heat two. Roberton damaged a brake pedal but added two points to his total. Both riders failed to score in the Yugoslavian GP, Davis having fuel feed troubles in heat one, and falling off in heat two. Roberton became mixed up with some wire fencing and then in the second leg collided with another rider, retiring with a broken throttle control.

There was a mysterious sequel to the Czechoslovakian GP, for Davis retired in both heats with complete fuel blockage. Somehow or other, sugar had been introduced into the petrol tank! Roberton managed to acquire eight points, putting him seventh in the table.

Following disagreement with AJS, Malcolm Davis was dropped from the team. Roberton was the sole representative in the Polish GP, but damaged a rear wheel in heat one and had engine bothers in the second leg.

We are not really concerned with the differences between Davis and AJS, but in *Motor Cycle* of June 4, 1969, quoting a TV interview, he stated that 'I was sacked'.

Davis' place was taken by Scotsman Jimmy Aird but misfortune plagued the team. Roberton broke two ribs following a crash at a Farleigh Castle scramble in May and, on May 18, Jimmy Aird fractured two bones in his right hand during a spill in the West German GP. With every top-line rider already committed to other factories, the AJS championship hopes for 1969 had faded almost to vanishing point. Private owners, of course, continued to record successes and, in the following chapter, the Y4 and 37-AT types are discussed.

Chapter 17

1969—and all that!

WITH THE ADVENT of the Y4, AJS was certainly ready for world markets. In the spring of 1969, the beautifully built scrambler had a highly enthusiastic reception in the USA, particularly on the West Coast where a new corporation had been formed to handle both AJS and Norton. Ever-increasing interest was also shown on the continent of Europe. The first Y4 to go to Holland was an outstanding success. In seven events, its Dutch rider took five first places. The Y4 was also supplemented by an entirely new trials model, the 37A-T, of which more anon.

In developing the Y4 prior to production, AJS adopted a policy of testing in actual competitions instead of the 'closed doors and secret tracks' used by many manufacturers. In truth, this was following the example of the Stevens brothers who had used a similar formula for introducing new machines.

There were heartbreaks, mistakes and mechanical failures—all of which occurred in full view of the public. However, every single failure or breakage was investigated thoroughly. Peter Inchley and his men were determined that when the Y4 reached the production stage it would be a meticulous engineering job, having the built-in reliability factor that had characterised the famous Ajay production bikes of the past.

Simplicity was a feature, the AJS technicians avoiding anything in the nature of added complication. Their aim was to build machines which could be used in event after event without the need for extensive overhauls and tedious stripping-down.

Although a power-output of 32 bhp could be made available, Peter Inchley calculated that 27 bhp at 6,400 rpm was ample and would increase the reliability factor, so essential in motocross events.

High-speed cine-photography and slow-motion cameras were employed in order to study the behaviour of suspension units in the most extreme conditions. These modern scientific methods have resulted in the remarkably efficient and wear-free lightweight 'Teledraulic' forks, and the Girling suspension units. Unsprung weight has also been drastically cut down by the adoption of ultra-light-weight AJS hubs and high-tensile-rim wheels.

To ensure absolute reliability in the transmission department, AJS engineers have employed an all-metal, diaphragm-type clutch, similar in design to that fitted on many high-performance and racing cars. The drive is taken through a close-ratio four-speed gearbox of immensely strong construction.

Trouble-free ignition is supplied by the energy-transfer system, consisting of a new-pattern coil, matched to an AC generator. This supplies a hefty spark right through the engine speed range. An Amal concentric type 932 carburettor has been modified specially for the Y4 AJS two-stroke engine. An air-cleaner is standardised, which actually aids the power-unit, as does the scientifically-designed exhaust system.

Detail has been studied throughout the design. The rear chain is easy and quick to adjust. Spring-loaded footrests are of the folding pattern; the hubs have an ingenious method of excluding dust and water, whilst weight is saved by the adoption of light-alloy mudguards and a two-gallon glass fibre petrol tank, finished in orange.

The seat has been evolved after consultation with the various AJS riders and is ideal for high-speed, cross-country riding. When one studies the frame, it is realised that this is a masterpiece of lightweight construction, possessing immense rigidity. Built from Reynolds 531 tubing, it is bronze-welded.

The AJS single-cylinder, two-stroke engine, developed from the original racing Starmaker unit, has a compression ratio of 12.3 to 1 and is built entirely from aluminium alloy, both barrel and crankcase being machined to the highest possible engineering standards. The cylinder is fitted with a spuncast iron liner for long-wearing properties. Piston, con rod and flywheels are individually balanced. Exceptionally good breathing characteristics produce excellent torque, particularly in the medium engine speed range. Bore and stroke are of 68 mm (2.67 inches), giving a displacement of 247 cc. The engine runs on a mixture of castor-based oil and premium petrol, in the proportion of 20 to 1.

With a dry weight of only a little over 200 lb, and a power output of 27 bhp, it is small wonder that the 250 cc Y4 AJS is a real flyer. This is equivalent to a power-weight ratio of nearly 300 bhp per ton! The two-stroke engine itself is giving

Right: Section through the timing side of the 250 cc AJS Y4 two-stroke power - unit, showing slightly convex piston crown, massive con-rod, double - roller big - end bearings, and energy transfer ignition system, with contact - breaker operated by cam on the engine shaft. Note also central location of sparking plug, and unique shape of combustion chamber.

Below: Basic frame of the Y4, comprising a top backbone (A) which absorbs all frame stresses, and a double loop structure to carry engine and gearbox. (B) takes all 'fore and aft' and tension loads. (C) takes all 'up-down' tension and compression loads. (D) are non-stressed members for carrying engine and accessories.

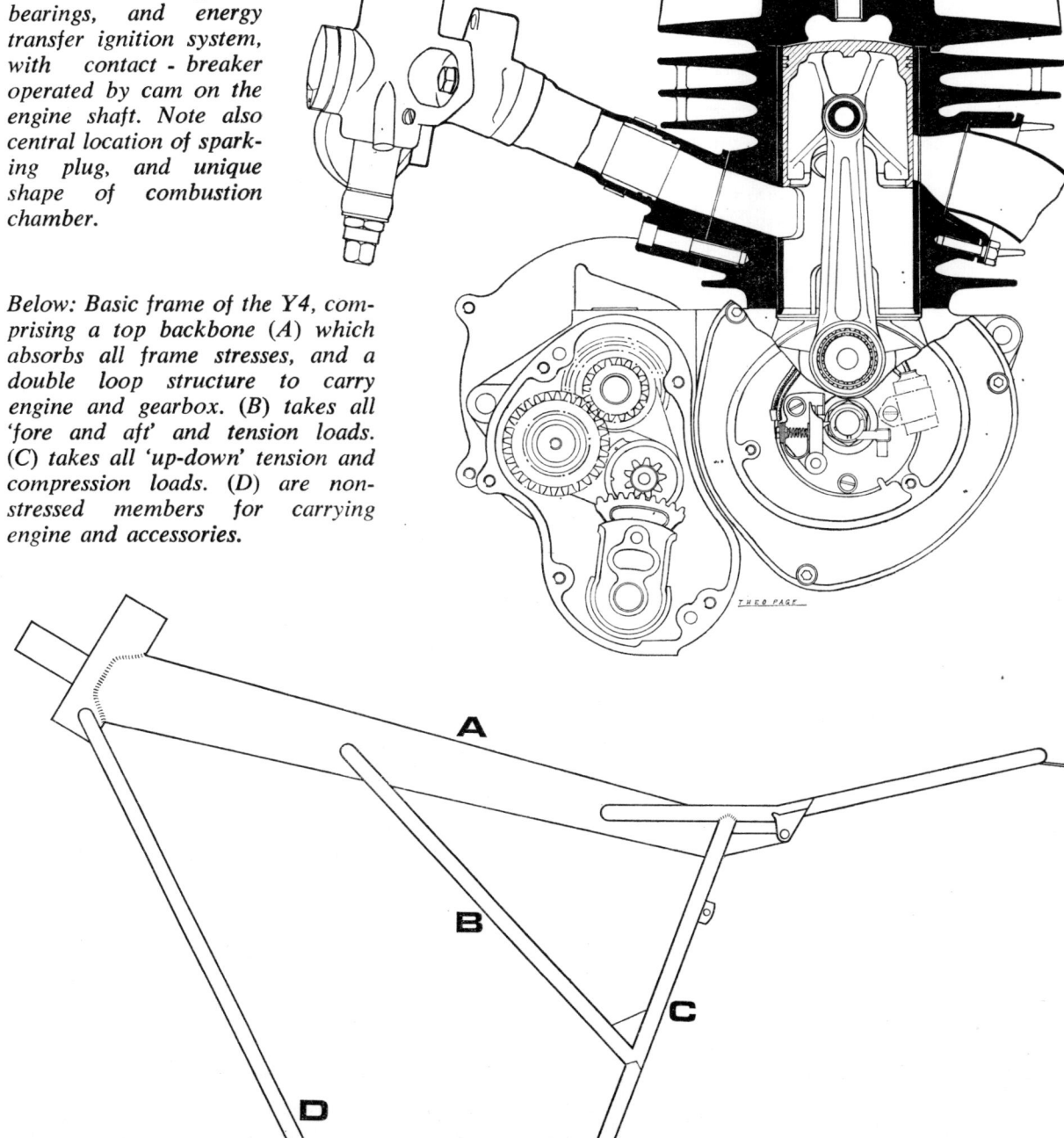

over 109 bhp per litre, a most commendable output for a production two-stroke 'single'.

As regards the AJS 37A-T trials bike, whilst this has much in common with the Y4 in general design, there are several differences. In the first place, torque is of far more importance than a high power output for mud-plugging, and the 246 cc Mark 37A engine is notable for its ability to slog at low speed in the stickiest of conditions. It produces 12.4 bhp at 5,000 rpm with a maximum torque of 16 lb/ft at 3,200 rpm, on a 7.9 to 1 compression ratio. Carburettor is a S25 Villiers unit, with renewable paper-filter element. The four-speed gearbox is manufactured by AJS and has ratios of 3.6, 2.4, 1.56 and 1.00 to 1.

A high-level exhaust system is used, the pipe being carried over the top of the engine, the silencer tucked neatly below the rider's seat and with adequate protection against burning the rider's legs.

The frame, based on that of the Y4, is built for AJS by Cotton Motorcycles Ltd from cold-drawn steel tubing. It is sifbronze-welded, with a tapered top-tube for maximum rigidity, and has a single down-tube. The forks are Metal Profile, designed to accept the continuous hammering which machines have to take in the devilish sections which are a feature of modern trials. Girling oil-damped units take care of the rear suspension and the swinging arms are constructed from $1\frac{1}{4}$ inch tubing, pivoted on 'lubricated-for-life' bearings.

AJS Y4 'SCRAMBLER'

Specification

Engine: Single-cylinder, aluminium-alloy AJS two-stroke 68 mm (2.676 inches) × 68 mm, 247 cc, 27 bhp at 6,400 rpm. Compression ratio 12.3 to 1. Gravity die-cast light-alloy piston with H6 22 cast-iron rings. Spun-cast-iron cylinder liner. Energy transfer ignition system (coil and AC generator). Champion N3 or Lodge RL49 sparking plug. Amal concentric Type 932 carburettor with special air-cleaner. Lubricated by castor-based oil mixed with premium-grade petrol, 20-1 ratio.

Frame: Immensely strong bronze-welded ultra-lightweight of Reynolds 531 tubing. Ultra-lightweight AJS Teledraulic forks, with $6\frac{1}{4}$ inch travel. Swinging-arm rear suspension controlled by Girling adjustable oil-damped units. Swinging-arms pivot on sealed-for-life polyurethane bushes, $3\frac{1}{4}$ inch spring travel. Light, forged-steel folding footrests, splined on to an adaptor, to give a wide range of adjustments.

Wheels, etc: High-tensile rims with 2.75-21 inch front, and 4.00-18 inch scrambler tyres. Ultra-lightweight AJS hubs, with special anti-dust and anti-water sealing. Light-alloy mudguards. Five-inch drum brakes, with riveted and bonded brake linings.

Transmission: All-metal, diaphragm clutch running in oil bath. Four-speed AJS gearbox, ratios: 2.03, 1.53, 1.255 and 1.00 to 1. Primary ratio (crankshaft/clutch) 20/43. Secondary (engine/rear wheel) 15/66-70-74. Gears running in oil bath (one pint). Quickly adjustable rear chain.

General: Two-gallon glass fibre petrol tank. Folding kick-starter. Competition pattern handlebars. Specially designed racing seat.

Dimensions, etc: Overall length, 83 inches; width, 34 inches; wheelbase, $55\frac{1}{2}$ inches; saddle height, 30 inches; ground clearance, $8\frac{1}{2}$ inches. Dry weight, 220 lb.

Makers: Norton Villiers Ltd, Andover, Hants, England.

AJS 37A-T

Specification

Engine: Two-stroke (66 mm × 72 mm), 246 cc. Compression ratio, 7.9 to 1. Cast-iron cylinder; 12.4 bhp at 5,000 rpm; maximum torque, 16 lb/ft at 3,200 rpm. Villiers S25 carburettor with renewable paper-element air filter. Flywheel magneto ignition.

Frame: Steel, cold-drawn tubing with tapered top tube; Sifbronze welded; single down tube. Swinging arm rear suspension of $1\frac{1}{4}$ inch tubing, pivoted on sealed-for-life nylon bushes; oil-damped Girling adjustable dampers. Metal Profile telescopic forks with progressive oil-damping.

Transmission: Four-speed, constant-mesh gearbox Ratios 3.6, 2.4, 1.56 and 1.00 to 1; 29 to 1 bottom gear (58T sprocket).

Wheels, etc: WM 1 × 21 (front) and WM 3 × 18 (rear); Dunlop trials tyres. Six inch light-alloy British Hub wheel centres, with cush drive in rear hub. 18 gauge light-alloy mudguards.

General: $1\frac{1}{4}$ gallon glass fibre petrol tank. High-level exhaust system with full protection for rider's legs. Special trials seat. Braced footrests with flat strip welded to the top and raised on the outer end for grip, in lightweight bar steel, drilled for lightness. Left-hand rest acts as rear-brake pivot point. Folding kick-starter. Trials-pattern handlebars.

Dimensions, etc: Wheelbase, $51\frac{1}{2}$ inches; saddle height, 30 inches; ground clearance, $9\frac{1}{2}$ inches. Weight (dry) 212 lb.

Makers: Norton Villiers Ltd, Andover, Hants, England.

Appendix 1

The AJS TT Riders—1911-1969

Listing rider's name, class, finishing position (R signifies retired) and date.

Name	Class	Pos.	Date
Ahearn, J.	Junior	17	1958
Aislabie, L. G.	,,	23	1955
Alexander, J.	,,	29	1956
	,,	29	1960
Anderson, H. R.	,,	R	1960
Anderson, J. D.	,,	R	1957
	,,	18	1958
Andersson, A.	,,	R	1967
	,,	R	1968
Andersson, A. V.	Senior	36	1961
	Junior	31	1961
	,,	21	1962
	Senior	R	1962
	Junior	30	1966
Andersson, S.	,,	R	1960
Anderton, S.	,,	41	1949
	,,	30	1950
	,,	26	1951
	,,	30	1952
Andrew, M.	,,	R	1967
Armstrong, H. R.	,,	5	1949
	Senior	4	1949
	Junior	23	1951
	Senior	R	1951
Ashton, J.	Junior	53	1969
Bailey, J.	,,	R	1955
Barnacle, G.	,,	18	1963
	,,	27	1964
	,,	29	1965
	,,	18	1966
	,,	18	1967
Barnett, A. J.	,,	R	1967
Barnett, S. T.	,,	R	1948
	,,	14	1949
	,,	17	1950
	Senior	36	1950
	Junior	19	1951
	,,	R	1952
	,,	25	1953
	,,	21	1954
Barrett, E. A.	,,	R	1951
	Senior	R	1951
Barrington, M.	Junior	39	1950
Barry, G. M. R.	,,	33	1969
Baxter, W. J.	,,	R	1967
	,,	40	1968
Baylie, R. W.	,,	23	1967
Begg, G. N.	,,	28	1956
	Senior	R	1956
Bell, C.	Junior	18	1926
Benson, W. G.	,,	R	1967
Black, N.	,,	R	1924
Blackler, C. V.	,,	5	1954
	Senior	R	1954
Blanchard, J.	Junior	6	1966
	,,	R	1967
Boardman, J. K.	,,	37	1951
Borland, G. A.	,,	33	1969
Boulton, W.	,,	R	1924
Boyce, E. F. H.	,,	8	1961
Boyce, E. F. H.	Junior	9	1962
Braine, E. W. J.	,,	65	1949
	,,	R	1950
Brett, J.	,,	R	1952
	Senior	R	1952
Brewster, D.	,,	R	1931
Brindley, J. D.	Junior	R	1957
Brown, A.	,,	56	1950
Brown, G.	,,	14	1951
	,,	6	1952
	,,	16	1953
Brown, R. E.	,,	60	1951
	,,	49	1953
Brown, R. N.	,,	46	1955
	,,	14	1958
Brown, T. R.	,,	R	1953
Brugiere, C. R.	,,	26	1951
	,,	R	1951
Bryen, K.	,,	13	1957
Burne, I.	,,	R	1968
Burne, I. M.	,,	18	1964
	,,	R	1965
Burt, A.	Senior	41	1958
	Junior	44	1958
	,,	34	1954
Burton, A. L.	,,	R	1956
Cameron, S. R.	,,	R	1956
	Senior	42	1956
	,,	R	1957
	Junior	47	1957
	,,	50	1959
Cann, M.	,,	5	1948
	,,	R	1952
Capper, R. C.	,,	R	1964
	,,	15	1965
	,,	R	1966
	,,	18	1969
Capstick, A.	,,	34	1968
	,,	48	1969
Carlsson, A.	,,	32	1962
	,,	13	1963
Carr, C. B.	,,	31	1954
	Senior	45	1954
	Junior	30	1955
Carr, L.	,,	18	1957
	,,	34	1959
	,,	30	1955
	,,	27	1960
	Senior	31	1961
	Junior	23	1961
	,,	R	1962
Carter, D. H.	,,	15	1948
Carter, P. H.	,,	11	1955
Catlin, G. A.	,,	10	1960
	,,	16	1961
Chambers, H.	,,	14	1922
	,,	R	1923
Chandler, R. S.	,,	13	1965
	,,	R	1967
Chapman, D. G.	,,	22	1955
Chapman, D. G.	Junior	36	1956
Chatterton, M.	,,	R	1967
Christian, D.	,,	11	1957
Christmas, N.	,,	R	1947
Clark, B. J.	,,	R	1967
Clark, H.	,,	10	1953
Clark, J. R.	,,	11	1953
	Senior	R	1953
	Junior	6	1954
	,,	R	1955
	,,	R	1956
Cohen, L. R. S.	,,	8	1927
	Senior	R	1927
	Junior	R	1928
	Senior	R	1928
Coleman, P. R.	Junior	R	1956
Coleman, R. W.	,,	8	1951
	,,	3	1952
	Senior	4	1952
	Junior	R	1953
Coleman, R. W.	Senior	4	1953
	Junior	1	1954
	Senior	R	1954
Collier, H. R.	Junior	58	1954
	,,	36	1955
Cooper, J. G.	,,	R	1968
Corke, J. D.	,,	15	1911
Cowan, E. R. H.	,,	36	1965
Crabtree, S. E.	Senior	17	1923
Croxford, D. L.	Junior	R	1965
	,,	R	1967
Cullingham, E. S.	,,	20	1938
	,,	R	1939
Dale, J. H.	,,	49	1950
Dale, R. H.	,,	R	1959
Daniell, H. L.	,,	R	1934
	Senior	9	1934
	Junior	8	1935
	Senior	R	1935
	Junior	9	1936
	Senior	R	1936
Davenport, L. H.	L/wght	R	1930
	Junior	10	1930
	Senior	R	1930
Davies, H. R.	Junior	R	1920
	Senior	R	1920
	Junior	2	1921
	Senior	1	1921
	Junior	R	1922
	Senior	R	1922
	Junior	R	1923
	Senior	R	1923
Davies, R.	Junior	R	1967
	,,	R	1968
Dawson, E.	,,	58	1953
Dear, L. A.	,,	Excl	1938
	,,	12	1948
	Senior	14	1948
	Junior	29	1949
	,,	R	1950

Name	Class	No.	Year
Dear, L. A,	Junior	R	1951
	,,	14	1952
	,,	28	1953
	,,	46	1954
De Kock, E. W.	,,	R	1965
Dent, J. B.	,,	71	1949
Denty, J. A.	,,	R	1967
Dickie, T.	,,	R	1967
Dickson, G. C.	,,	27	1963
Doran, W.	,,	27	1948
	,,	R	1949
	Senior	8	1949
	Junior	R	1951
	Senior	2	1951
	Junior	5	1953
	Senior	5	1953
Driver, E. G.	Junior	9	1964
	,,	9	1965
	,,	R	1963
Duckett, V. F.	,,	20	1966
	,,	19	1967
Duff, M. A.	,,	15	1961
	,,	5	1962
	,,	6	1963
	,,	3	1964
	,,	R	1965
	,,	R	1967
Dugdale, A.	,,	43	1961
	,,	44	1962
Duncan, B.	,,	35	1965
Duncan, D. J.	,,	R	1963
	,,	29	1964
	,,	28	1966
Dunlop, G.	,,	12	1963
Dunn, C. A.	Senior	48	1958
	Junior	R	1958
Ebert, H.	,,	R	1964
Eccles, G. C.	,,	R	1962
Ekstrom, H.	,,	R	1960
Ellis, D. J.	,,	30	1963
Ellerby, C.	,,	38	1954
	L/wght	R	1955
	Junior	43	1955
Ennett, D.	,,	7	1955
	,,	2	1956
Evans, E. R.	,,	R	1939
	,,	30	1949
	,,	20	1952
	,,	22	1954
Evans, P. R.	,,	R	1961
	,,	R	1962
Evans, W.	,,	61	1949
	L/wght	R	1950
	,,	11	1951
	Junior	41	1951
Fagerstrom, F. O.	,,	48	1960
Fahey, P. B.	,,	R	1956
Fairbairn, F.	,,	51	1949
	,,	R	1950
Farrant, D. K.	,,	6	1953
	,,	2	1954
	Senior	R	1954
Featherstone, W. S.	Junior	4	1951
	Senior	R	1951
Fenn, R. A.	Junior	52	1949
Fenning, L. F. M.	,,	73	1949
Ferguson, R.	Junior	38	1953
	Senior	R	1955
	Junior	R	1956
	,,	R	1957
	,,	41	1958
Filler, D.	,,	29	1968
Fisher, J.	,,	39	1952
	Senior	35	1952
	Junior	R	1953
	Senior	33	1953
	Junior	49	1954
Fletcher, J.	,,	50	1949
Flury, L.	Senior	R	1958
	Junior	35	1958
Fogarty, G. C.	,,	12	1966
Fogarty, G. L.	,,	R	1967
	,,	R	1968
Foll, R.	,,	R	1962
	,,	15	1964
Foster, A. R.	,,	R	1937
	,,	R	1938
	Senior	R	1938
	Junior	R	1938
	Senior	13	1939
Fox, R. E.	F1 (350)	12	1959
	Senior	R	1959
	Junior	4	1959
Francis, C. H.	,,	R	1948
	,,	R	1949
'Franklen, S.'	,,	R	1951
	Senior	16	1951
	Junior	R	1952
	Senior	R	1952
	Junior	R	1952
	Senior	30	1953
Frend, E. J.	Junior	R	1948
	Senior	R	1948
	Junior	8	1949
	Senior	R	1949
	Junior	5	1950
	Senior	15	1950
	Junior	R	1953
Fulton, W.	,,	49	1969
Gallagher, D.	,,	11	1966
	,,	15	1967
	,,	12	1968
Gate, U.	,,	R	1955
Gilbert, L. D.	,,	R	1951
	,,	R	1952
	,,	40	1953
	Senior	31	1953
Gill, T. R.	Junior	R	1967
Glazebrook, A. J.	,,	R	1950
	,,	R	1952
	,,	27	1953
	,,	41	1954
	,,	R	1955
	Senior	38	1957
	Junior	48	1957
	L/wght	R	1961
Gow, J.	Junior	R	1965
Graham, L. S.	,,	37	1964
Graham, R. L.	Senior	9	1947
	Junior	7	1948
	Senior	R	1948
	Junior	R	1949
Graham, R. L.	Junior	4	1950
	Senior	4	1950
Granath, B.	Junior	R	1963
	,,	R	1965
Gray, C.	,,	56	1949
	,,	23	1950
	Senior	30	1950
	Junior	24	1951
	Senior	18	1951
	Junior	32	1952
	Senior	41	1952
	Junior	21	1953
	Senior	27	1953
Griffin, A. W.	Junior	R	1929
Griffiths, G.	,,	6	1969
Griffiths, S. G.	,,	R	1967
	,,	R	1968
Grinton, G.	,,	2	1922
Guthrie, A. J.	L/wght	1	1930
	Junior	R	1930
	Senior	R	1930
Haddock, B.	Junior	6	1914
Haddow, D.	,,	17	1963
Hailwood, S. M. B.	,,	R	1960
	,,	R	1961
Haldane, R. C.	,,	40	1965
Handley, W. L.	,,	2	1929
	Senior	R	1929
Harding, J.	Junior	59	1951
	,,	42	1952
Hardy, E. V. C.	,,	52	1952
	Senior	38	1952
	Junior	36	1953
	Senior	28	1953
Harris, H. F.	Junior	R	1920
	,,	8	1921
	Senior	14	1921
	Junior	R	1922
	,,	2	1923
	Senior	R	1923
Harrison, R.	Junior	25	1952
Harrison, R. E. D.	,,	R	1951
Harrowell, D. W. J.	,,	26	1949
	,,	20	1950
Hartley, H.	,,	30	1948
Harwood, C. K. W.	,,	R	1951
	,,	R	1952
Hawken, F. C.	,,	13	1950
	,,	20	1951
Hay, I. M.	,,	38	1949
Hayden, G. H.	,,	44	1949
	,,	31	1950
Heanski, J. H. D.	,,	R	1960
Heath, F. P.	,,	37	1949
	,,	R	1952
	,,	R	1954
	Senior	R	1954
Heaton, W. M.	Junior	10	1913
	,,	29	1914
Hewartson, D. P.	,,	37	1963
Hewartson, P.	,,	R	1964
Hicks, F. G.	,,	R	1930
	,,	R	1931
	Senior	R	1931
Higgins, F. J.	Junior	28	1958
Himing, G.	,,	8	1930

Name	Class	No.	Year
Himing, G.	Senior	12	1930
	Junior	14	1931
Hobson, M.	,,	41	1962
	,,	20	1963
	,,	44	1965
Hodgkin, J. P. E.	,,	53	1949
	,,	R	1950
Holdsworth, T. T.	,,	18	1965
Hollowell, J. W.	,,	R	1923
	Senior	R	1923
Hough, C. W.	Junior	R	1923
	Senior	20	1923
	Junior	R	1924
	Senior	6	1924
	Junior	4	1925
	Senior	R	1925
	Junior	7	1926
	Senior	R	1926
	Junior	R	1927
	Senior	11	1927
Houseley, E.	Junior	9	1954
Howard, O.	,,	R	1964
Hunt, C. W.	,,	29	1963
Hunter, A. R. C.	,,	R	1964
	,,	11	1965
	,,	R	1966
Hunter, B. W.	,,	R	1968
Inchley, P.	L/wght	R	1967
Ivy, W. D.	Junior	R	1965
Jackson, S. P.	,,	13	1927
	Senior	R	1927
Jarman, D.	,,	27	1961
	Junior	33	1961
Jefferies, A.	,,	22	1969
Jenkins, G. A.	,,	14	1964
Jensen, S. H.	,,	12	1949
	,,	16	1950
Johansson, K.	,,	39	1953
Johnson, E. A.	,,	42	1962
Johnston, S. A.	,,	50	1969
Jones, A. W.	,,	30	1954
	,,	50	1955
	,,	R	1956
	Senior	34	1957
	Junior	30	1957
Jones, W.	,,	4	1914
Julian, C.	,,	17	1953
Kay, K.	,,	36	1963
	,,	42	1965
	,,	29	1966
	,,	25	1967
Kellas, A. C.	,,	43	1951
	,,	67	1952
Kelly, G.	,,	4	1921
	,,	R	1922
	Senior	R	1922
	Junior	14	1923
Kentish, J. F.	,,	29	1950
	,,	40	1951
	Senior	25	1951
Keys, B. E.	Junior	R	1948
	L/wght	R	1949
King, A.	Junior	R	1962
Klein, M.	,,	53	1950
	,,	48	1951
	Senior	30	1951
Langston, R. J.	Junior	R	1961
Laurent, R. J.	,,	22	1953
Lawton, S.	,,	20	1948
	Senior	R	1948
	Junior	13	1949
	,,	18	1950
	Senior	20	1951
	Junior	R	1951
	,,	5	1952
	Senior	12	1952
Lee, D.	Junior	37	1965
	,,	13	1966
	,,	R	1967
Lee, R.	,,	35	1950
	Senior	41	1950
Lenz, E.	Junior	32	1965
Lind, J. G.	L/wght	5	1930
	Junior	11	1930
	Senior	9	1930
Lindsay, K. A.	Junior	51	1969
Lishman, J. B.	,,	R	1967
Lloyd, I. I.	,,	24	1954
Lockwood, M. V.	,,	24	1950
	,,	R	1951
	Senior	R	1951
	Junior	R	1952
Lomas, W. A.	,,	4	1952
	Senior	5	1952
Longman, F. A.	Junior	R	1922
	,,	6	1923
	,,	R	1924
	Senior	8	1924
	Junior	R	1925
	Sidecar	4	1925
	Senior	2	1925
	Junior	8	1926
	Senior	3	1926
	Junior	R	1929
	Senior	16	1929
Low, M. E.	Junior	7	1963
Lund, B.	,,	R	1965
	,,	21	1966
	,,	R	1967
Lund, G.	,,	61	1951
Lunde, M. C.	,,	R	1967
	,,	R	1968
Lyons, E.	,,	16	1948
MacDonald, R. L.	Senior	52	1950
	Junior	57	1951
	Senior	38	1951
	Junior	43	1952
	Senior	40	1952
	Junior	50	1953
	Senior	34	1953
Mahoney, P. M.	Junior	35	1968
Marcotte, J. R.	Senior	40	1958
	Junior	46	1958
Marston, F. R.	,,	9	1924
Martin, A. F. G. D.	,,	30	1955
	,,	R	1956
	,,	42	1957
McAlpine, W. A.	,,	13	1951
McConnell, R. D.	,,	R	1951
McCosh, W.	Senior	32	1960
	Junior	43	1960
	,,	22	1961
McCosh, W.	Junior	18	1962
	,,	28	1963
	,,	16	1964
	,,	R	1965
	,,	R	1966
McCosh, W. M.	,,	11	1967
McCutcheon, N. C.	,,	9	1957
McDonald, R.	,,	74	1949
McEwan, T.	,,	R	1950
McGeagh, M. R.	,,	50	1954
McGurk, A.	,,	R	1967
	,,	R	1968
McIntyre, R.	,,	R	1953
	Senior	14	1954
	Junior	R	1959
	,,	R	1960
McPherson, E.	,,	11	1949
	Senior	14	1949
	Junior	R	1950
	Senior	14	1950
McStay, W. M.	Junior	25	1966
Meagan, W. H. T.	,,	R	1927
Meehan, C.	,,	R	1962
Millard, S. M.	,,	R	1967
Miller, S. M.	,,	R	1950
	,,	R	1951
	,,	R	1952
Mizen, W. S.	,,	25	1958
	,,	15	1959
	,,	11	1960
	,,	R	1961
	,,	R	1962
	,,	4	1963
	,,	8	1964
	,,	12	1965
Mooney, M.	,,	R	1950
Moore, C. V.	,,	20	1937
Morton, J. D.	,,	31	1962
	,,	50	1964
Moyle, A. J.	,,	R	1924
	Senior	R	1924
Mudford, K. H.	Junior	18	1951
	Senior	R	1951
	Junior	R	1952
	,,	7	1953
Munro, J. I.	,,	22	1968
Murdoch, G. G.	,,	37	1948
	Senior	4	1948
Murphy, G. A.	Junior	8	1953
	,,	43	1954
	,,	R	1955
Murray, S.	,,	36	1960
Myers, H. B.	,,	48	1948
	,,	R	1949
Neeve, C.	,,	R	1968
Nelson, B.	,,	R	1964
Neve, C.	,,	36	1967
Newman, G.	,,	14	1948
Norris, F. A.	,,	R	1953
	,,	43	1954
	,,	R	1955
	,,	20	1956
Nygren, O.	,,	R	1921
Olsson, V.	,,	15	1953
O'Rourke, M. P.	,,	27	1954
	,,	R	1960

Name	Class	No.	Year
Palmer, P.	Junior	33	1956
Pantlin, E.	,,	40	1955
Parker, R. V.	,,	R	1967
Parkinson, R. F.	,,	R	1927
	Senior	15	1927
	Junior	R	1928
	,,	R	1929
Parsonage, C. A.	,,	R	1967
Parsons, L. W.	,,	R	1949
Pawson, P. G. R.	,,	R	1959
	,,	R	1960
Paterson, G. L.	,,	10	1948
	,,	22	1949
	,,	25	1950
	Senior	31	1950
	Junior	16	1951
	Senior	19	1951
	Junior	24	1953
Pepper, J. R.	,,	R	1967
Perris, F. G.	,,	8	1956
Petch, C. W.	,,	R	1949
	,,	R	1950
	,,	15	1951
Petty, R. J. A.	,,	47	1949
Pike, R. H.	,,	R	1948
	,,	22	1949
	,,	14	1950
Plews, H.	,,	28	1955
	,,	44	1957
	Senior	R	1959
	Junior	35	1959
Pollitt, J. A.	,,	45	1953
Powell, D. T.	,,	18	1955
	,,	7	1956
	,,	18	1959
	,,	18	1960
	,,	14	1961
	,,	15	1962
Pratt, R.	,,	42	1953
Prescott, H. V.	,,	8	1920
Prince, K. R. E.	,,	R	1953
	Senior	29	1953
Proctor, B. G.	Junior	12	1965
Purnell, J. E. C.	,,	36	1949
Purslow, B. G.	,,	R	1953
Purvis, S. G.	,,	21	1961
	,,	19	1962
Ransom, H. B.	,,	28	1950
	Senior	38	1950
	Junior	22	1951
	Senior	26	1951
	Junior	19	1952
Ransome, L. B.	,,	59	1950
	Senior	48	1950
	Junior	34	1953
	Senior	32	1953
	Junior	37	1956
	,,	49	1957
	,,	49	1959
Rayner, H. W.	,,	19	1963
	,,	32	1964
	,,	26	1965
	,,	22	1966
	,,	R	1967
Read, P. W.	,,	2	1964
Richter, L.	,,	R	1959
Righton, J.	Junior	37	1959
Riley, H.	,,	24	1962
Ring, E.	,,	8	1952
	,,	R	1953
Robarts, G.	,,	R	1955
Robertson, W.	Senior	40	1961
	Junior	36	1961
	,,	12	1962
	Senior	R	1962
Rood, B. W. T.	Junior	4	1953
Rowbottom, R. A.	,,	R	1952
	Senior	R	1952
	Junior	R	1953
	Senior	R	1953
	Junior	28	1954
	,,	R	1955
Rowley, G.	,,	R	1925
	,,	R	1926
	Senior	6	1926
	Junior	R	1927
	Senior	9	1927
	Junior	R	1928
	Senior	2	1928
	,,	R	1929
	Junior	9	1931
	Senior	R	1931
	Junior	11	1934
	Senior	12	1934
	Junior	13	1935
	Senior	R	1935
	Junior	10	1936
	Senior	R	1936
	Junior	8	1937
	,,	R	1938
	,,	23	1939
Rusk, W. F.	Senior	11	1939
Rutherford, R. S.	Junior	26	1958
Salt, G. T.	,,	R	1959
	,,	7	1960
Sandry, C. W.	,,	R	1967
	,,	14	1968
Sapsford, B.	,,	R	1967
	,,	R	1968
Saward, G.	,,	26	1964
Schimpf, P. L.	,,	R	1962
Scott, G.	,,	14	1953
	Senior	23	1953
Shaw, A. E.	Junior	R	1949
Shaw, R.	,,	38	1963
Sheard, T. M.	,,	R	1920
	,,	3	1921
	,,	1	1922
	,,	R	1923
Shepherd, A.	,,	R	1959
	,,	7	1960
	,,	R	1961
	,,	35	1962
	,,	12	1963
Shepherd, T. S.	,,	R	1954
	Senior	31	1954
Sherry, R. H.	Junior	R	1953
	Senior	8	1953
Shorey, D. F.	Junior	28	1963
	,,	33	1964
Simcock, A. E.	,,	R	1927
	Senior	R	1927
Simister, T.	Senior	R	1931
Simpson, J. H.	Junior	R	1923
	,,	R	1924
	,,	3	1925
	Sidecar	5	1925
	Senior	R	1925
	Junior	2	1926
	Senior	R	1926
	Junior	3	1927
	Senior	R	1927
	Junior	R	1928
	Senior	R	1928
Simpson, L. T.	Junior	13	1953
	,,	4	1954
Slater, J. S.	,,	R	1949
	,,	34	1950
	,,	34	1951
	,,	35	1952
Smith, D. W.	,,	29	1961
	,,	R	1962
	Senior	21	1962
Smith, W. A.	Junior	29	1958
	,,	17	1959
	,,	12	1961
	,,	13	1962
	,,	10	1965
	,,	10	1966
	,,	14	1967
Spann, T.	,,	R	1928
	Senior	13	1928
	Junior	15	1929
	Senior	R	1929
	,,	R	1931
Standing, R.	Junior	39	1964
	,,	38	1965
	,,	R	1966
	,,	20	1967
Starr, L.	Senior	27	1951
	Junior	28	1952
	Senior	29	1952
	Junior	R	1953
Steele, R. N.	,,	R	1967
Stephen, H. L.	,,	R	1953
Stevens, A. J.	,,	16	1911
Stevens, C. A.	,,	19	1949
	,,	R	1950
	Senior	R	1950
	Junior	R	1951
Stevens, F. J.	Senior	19	1959
	Junior	39	1959
	,,	12	1964
	,,	12	1965
Stevens, J. H.	,,	19	1926
	Senior	R	1926
Stevenson, D. S.	Junior	44	1952
	,,	31	1952
Stidolph, F. E.	,,	46	1951
Stirling, J.	,,	R	1923
Storr, W. C.	,,	43	1950
	,,	43	1951
Swallow, K. W.	,,	33	1952
	,,	R	1953
	Senior	R	1953
	Junior	44	1955
Swarbrick, T. W.	,,	R	1953
Tait, P. H.	,,	15	1955

Name	Category	No.	Year
Taylor, J.	Junior	20	1968
Taylor, J. B.	,,	27	1967
Tedder, L. G.	,,	R	1952
	Senior	R	1952
Thomas, E. R.	Junior	R	1938
Thomson, R. G.	,,	4	1955
	,,	34	1956
	,,	34	1957
	,,	R	1958
Thorp, T.	,,	R	1960
	,,	R	1961
Thorp, T.	,,	13	1962
Tompsett, J. L.	Senior	45	1958
	Junior	43	1958
Tully, K. E.	,,	48	1952
	,,	R	1955
Tyrell-Smith H. G.	,,	R	1934
	Senior	7	1934
	Junior	10	1935
Varlow, J.	,,	45	1950
	,,	35	1951
	Senior	R	1951
	Junior	34	1952
Wade, J. E.	,,	15	1927
	Senior	R	1927
	Junior	R	1928
Wade, O.	,,	R	1920
	,,	6	1921
Wade, O.	Senior	12	1922
	Junior	R	1924
Wales, J. A.	,,	R	1966
Walker, G. J.	,,	R	1953
Walker, W. B.	,,	R	1950
	,,	55	1951
Walmsley, B.	,,	30	1966
	,,	23	1968
Walmsley, S.	,,	22	1967
Walton, F.	,,	28	1963
	,,	R	1968
Weiss, E.	,,	R	1964
	,,	R	1966
West, J. M.	,,	R	1933
	Senior	14	1947
	Junior	13	1948
	Senior	R	1948
Wheeler, A. F.	Junior	19	1953
	,,	10	1954
	Senior	28	1954
	Junior	12	1955
	Senior	35	1958
	Junior	R	1958
	Senior	R	1959
	Junior	21	1959
Whiteside, E.	,,	40	1961
	,,	37	1962
Wildman, D. J.	Senior	35	1961
Wildman, D. J.	Junior	41	1961
	,,	20	1962
Williams, C.	,,	R	1913
	,,	2	1914
	,,	1	1920
Williams, D.	,,	22	1964
Williams, E.	,,	1	1914
	,,	R	1920
	,,	1	1921
Williams, J.	,,	15	1969
Williams, J. H.	,,	36	1964
	,,	23	1965
Williams, P. J.	,,	2	1966
	,,	R	1967
	,,	21	1968
Williams, S. M.	,,	R	1925
	Senior	R	1925
	,,	R	1930
Willis, K.	,,	33	1953
	,,	49	1954
Wise, C. E.	Junior	R	1926
	Senior	17	1926
Wood, J. J.	Junior	23	1958
Woodman, D.	,,	10	1962
	,,	8	1963
	,,	5	1964
Young, C. P.	,,	26	1961
Young, L. P.	,,	22	1958

Appendix 2

The Amateur TT and Manx GP Riders—1923-1968

Listing rider's name, class, finishing position (R signifies retired) and date.
Abbreviation N indicates Newcomers' race and SN Snaefell Course.

Name	Class	Pos	Year
Abbey, J. R.	Junior	R	1962
Ablett, I.	„	R	1961
	„	R	1962
	„	30	1963
Adams, R. D.	—	1	1926
Alcock, G. D.	Junior	29	1957
	Senior	41	1957
'Alexander, J.'	Junior	11	1951
	„	R	1952
	„	26	1953
Alexander, P. A.	„	R	1955
Allott, M. L.	„	33	1968
Anderton, S.	„	11	1948
Andrews, E.	„	17	1951
Antill, D. P. L.	Senior	14	1954
Appleyard, C. B.	Junior	R	1958
	Senior	51	1958
	Junior	64	1959
Archard, N. G.	„	31	1962
	„	42	1963
	„	11	1967
Armstrong, H. R.	„	R	1948
Armstrong, J.	„	R	1964
Arnold, M. D.	„	35	1954
	Senior	R	1954
	Junior	29	1955
	Senior	R	1955
	Junior	51	1957
Arter, T. E.	„	14	1938
Ashton, G. O. W.	—	R	1925
Ashton, J.	Junior	36	1964
	„	31	1965
Avis, A. S.	Jnr (N)	19	1957
	„	46	1957
Bagshawe, P.	„	43	1952
	Senior	44	1952
Bailey, M. J.	Junior	R	1968
Bancroft, M.	„	R	1960
	„	36	1961
	„	16	1962
	„	19	1963
Barnacle, G.	„	33	1961
	„	21	1962
Barnes, E. W.	Jnr (SN)	35	1958
Barnett, A. J.	Junior	R	1964
	„	10	1965
Bassett, A. D.	„	29	1951
	Senior	R	1951
Baylie, R. W.	Junior	57	1965
Begg, G. N.	„	25	1955
	Senior	25	1955
Bell, G.	Junior	15	1959
	„	6	1961
	„	R	1962
	„	R	1963
Bennett, B. A.	„	35	1961
	„	R	1962

Name	Class	Pos	Year
Bennison, W.	Junior	50	1948
Bent, H.	„	R	1956
	„	60	1957
Bethell, R.	„	R	1964
Bevan, W. G.	„	8	1929
Bilsborrow, E.	„	23	1968
Bilsborrow, R.	„	21	1967
Birch, W. L.	„	R	1929
Bird, M. R.	„	47	1967
	„	R	1968
Bisbey, R.	„	R	1959
	„	R	1960
Blair, J. S.	Senior	59	1951
	Junior	13	1952
	Senior	21	1952
Bloomfield, F. A.	Junior	R	1963
Boult, L. D.	„	55	1952
	Senior	59	1952
Boyce, E. F. H.	Junior	15	1953
	Senior	R	1953
Braidwood, W. S.	—	R	1925
	—	R	1926
Bramhall, N.	Snr (SN)	5	1958
	Junior	R	1958
Brown, J. K.	„	51	1968
Brassington, A. R.	„	R	1948
	„	18	1949
	„	12	1950
	„	32	1951
	„	34	1952
Brazier, V. R.	Jnr (N)	41	1957
Bretherton, H.	Junior	R	1937
	„	R	1938
	Senior	R	1938
Bridgham, H.	—	R	1926
Briggs, G. E.	Senior	44	1960
Brilton, D. F.	Junior	44	1965
Broadley, A. L.	„	40	1953
	Senior	35	1953
	Junior	66	1955
	Senior	55	1955
Brocklington, P. C.	—	12	1927
Brown, A.	Junior	R	1949
Brown, A. D.	„	13	1950
	„	31	1951
	Senior	R	1951
	Junior	40	1952
Brown, T. W.	„	47	1952
	Senior	45	1952
Buchan, G. B.	Junior	13	1963
Buchanan, J. H.	„	R	1960
	„	50	1962
Bucknall, A. G.	„	R	1931
Bury, L. J.	Senior	R	1959
	Junior	R	1960
Butcher, A. J.	„	33	1953
	Senior	30	1953

Name	Class	Pos	Year
Butcher, A. J.	Junior	40	1954
	Senior	31	1954
Buxton, N. E.	Junior	51	1951
	„	63	1952
	Senior	60	1952
Byrne, J. E.	Junior	R	1928
	Senior	R	1928
Cammack, B.	Junior	36	1965
	„	37	1967
Capper, R. C.	„	34	1963
Carman, R. H.	„	33	1954
	Senior	R	1954
	Junior	22	1955
	Senior	29	1955
	„	27	1957
	Junior	14	1958
	Senior	13	1958
	Junior	R	1959
	Senior	26	1959
Carr, P.	Junior	32	1954
	Senior	R	1954
	Junior	R	1955
	Senior	41	1955
	Junior	R	1958
Castle, R.	„	79	1959
Challis, M. C.	„	R	1956
Chambers, R.	Jnr (SN)	60	1958
Chandler, R. S.	Junior	15	1963
	„	R	1964
Chapman, J.	„	45	1962
	„	29	1963
	„	14	1964
Chivers, C. A.	Jnr (N)	34	1957
	Senior	41	1960
	Junior	R	1962
Christian, D.	„	R	1955
Clark, G. D.	„	28	1952
	Senior	R	1952
Clark, H.	Junior	2	1952
Clarke, A. E.	Jnr (N)	36	1957
	Jnr (SN)	44	1958
Clarke, I.	Junior	R	1957
Clarkson, D.	„	R	1968
Collett, G. E.	„	R	1953
	Senior	R	1953
Collings, A. C. R.	Junior	57	1949
Collison, A. H.	„	R	1935
Cook, R. G.	„	R	1955
	Senior	R	1955
Cooper, S.	„	40	1950
Cope, E. F.	L/wght	R	1948
	Junior	51	1949
	Senior	R	1949
Corfield, W.	Junior	R	1933
	Senior	R	1933
	Junior	R	1934
Corlett, G. E.	„	45	1959

Name	Grade	No.	Year
Corlett, G. E.	Junior	27	1960
Corley, W. J.	„	39	1949
	Senior	44	1949
Cortoriend, R. B.	Junior	51	1954
Cowles, R. J.	„	55	1963
Crann, R. G.	„	65	1956
	„	61	1957
Crebbin, P. T.	„	29	1949
	Senior	22	1949
Crooks, E. B.	Junior	R	1952
	„	13	1953
	„	8	1954
Crossley, D. G.	„	3	1949
	„	1	1950
Croucher, V. F. G.	Jnr (N)	51	1957
Crowder, H.	Junior	R	1959
Crowther, R. G.	„	R	1967
Cruse, P. K.	„	42	1955
	Senior	R	1955
Culshaw, A.	Jnr (N)	30	1957
Cunliffe, J. O.	Junior	64	1951
Cupples, R. F.	—	R	1926
Dakin, P. L.	Junior	43	1955
	Senior	52	1955
	Junior	R	1956
	Senior	30	1956
	Junior	R	1957
	Senior	21	1957
Dallow, J.	Junior	R	1967
	„	R	1968
Daniels, G. J.	„	R	1967
	„	13	1968
Darvill, P. J.	„	19	1959
	„	R	1961
	„	2	1962
	„	1	1963
Davenport, A. F.	„	67	1949
	„	49	1950
	Senior	62	1950
Davey, P. A.	Junior	12	1962
Davies, E. P.	„	R	1958
Davis, B. J.	„	R	1964
	„	8	1965
Davis, J. D. O.	Senior	55	1950
Dawson, J.	Junior	26	1968
Dawson, R. P.	„	37	1959
	„	5	1960
	„	2	1961
	„	1	1962
Daykin, D. R.	Jnr (N)	40	1957
Deakin, R. C.	Junior	20	1968
Degens, D. F.	„	R	1964
Dent, J. D.	„	37	1948
Denty, J. A.	„	43	1963
	„	R	1964
Dicker, D. J.	„	30	1960
	„	21	1961
	„	18	1962
	„	18	1963
Dickie, T.	„	R	1965
Dickson, G. C.	„	52	1962
Dodsworth, J. M.	„	R	1967
Downes, G. T.	„	38	1956
	Senior	36	1956
	„	R	1957
	Junior	R	1958
Downes, G. T.	Senior	36	1958
Dowty, R.	Junior	R	1953
Drysdale, I. D.	„	25	1948
Drysdale, J.	„	R	1955
	„	8	1956
Duckert, V. F.	„	R	1962
Duncan, D. J.	„	21	1959
Duncan, J. C.	Senior	R	1950
	Junior	18	1951
	„	22	1952
	„	11	1953
	Senior	19	1953
Dunlop, G. R.	Junior	24	1953
	Senior	20	1953
	Junior	15	1954
	„	R	1955
Dunphy, P. J.	„	R	1962
East, C.	„	50	1965
Edwards, C. R.	„	70	1959
Edwards, G.	„	44	1948
	„	37	1949
	Senior	R	1949
Ellerby, C.	Junior	33	1952
Elmore, P. N.	„	R	1967
	„	6	1968
Ennett, D.	„	4	1952
	Senior	5	1952
	Junior	R	1953
	„	1	1954
Evans, G.	„	R	1961
	„	47	1962
	„	56	1963
	„	25	1964
	„	R	1967
	„	R	1968
Evans, L. E.	„	69	1955
Ewer, G. N.	„	R	1950
	„	33	1951
Fairbairn, F.	„	16	1948
Farrant, D. K.	„	3	1952
	Senior	1	1952
Fawkes, J. N.	Junior	40	1956
Fiedler, C.	„	62	1963
	„	R	1964
	„	33	1965
Fisher, C. R.	„	R	1950
	Senior	R	1950
Fleet, J. A.	„	R	1928
	Junior	17	1930
Fletcher, A. H.	„	R	1964
Fletcher, F.	„	R	1949
Flury, L.	„	54	1956
	Senior	R	1956
	Junior	R	1957
	Senior	53	1957
Fox, R.	Junior	64	1963
	„	42	1964
	„	R	1965
Fox, R. E.	Jnr (SN)	2	1958
	Senior	R	1958
'Franklin, S.'	Junior	R	1948
	„	9	1949
	Senior	24	1949
Frost, A. H.	Junior	47	1955
	Senior	49	1955
	Junior	64	1956
Fulton, G.	Junior	27	1967
	„	31	1968
Fulton, W.	„	5	1964
	„	18	1965
Gallagher, D. J.	„	29	1948
Gates, R. W. F.	„	R	1962
	„	51	1963
	„	33	1964
	„	42	1965
Gilchrist, A. J. G.	—	R	1925
Gill, A. B.	Senior	R	1959
Goddard, I. R.	Junior	R	1961
	„	42	1962
Godfrey, T.	„	5	1959
Goodwin, E.	„	32	1953
	Senior	R	1953
	Junior	50	1954
	„	63	1956
Graham, E.	„	49	1951
Graham, R. A.	„	12	1967
Gray, A.	„	R	1964
Greenwood, O. E.	Senior	10	1954
	Junior	12	1955
Griffiths, C. G.	Senior	40	1949
	Junior	9	1950
	„	20	1957
	Senior	27	1957
Griffiths, J. T.	Junior	19	1961
	„	32	1962
	„	24	1963
Griffiths, S. G.	„	22	1961
	„	4	1962
	„	3	1963
	„	R	1964
Haddock, R. F.	„	R	1968
Haldane, E. McG.	„	19	1955
Hall, G.	„	R	1948
Hall, P. M.	„	16	1951
	Senior	R	1951
	Junior	25	1952
	Senior	22	1952
	Junior	22	1954
	Senior	16	1954
Hamilton, J. D.	Jnr (N)	R	1957
Harding, R. M.	„	26	1955
	Senior	20	1955
Harding, W.	Junior	57	1947
	„	31	1953
Harper, H. J.	„	R	1968
Harris, R.	„	R	1930
Harrison, D. R.	„	R	1968
Hartle, J.	„	21	1953
Heath, F. P.	„	2	1948
Hedley, J.	„	67	1952
Henderson, F. W.	„	R	1968
Henderson, G.	„	35	1950
Henson, J. T.	„	47	1964
	„	13	1965
Herbert, A. S.	„	31	1949
	Senior	20	1949
	Junior	19	1950
Herrod, D.	„	R	1955
Hewison, E. F.	—	R	1926
Hickson, A.	Junior	R	1952
Hilton, V. E.	„	50	1964
Hodgson, A. L.	„	R	1930

Newstead, A.	Junior	20	1956	Pilling, D.	Junior	58	1963	Roberts, C. A. H.	Junior	62	1948
	,,	18	1957	Pinckard, A. D.	Senior	56	1950	Robertson, J. S.	,,	59	1948
	,,	15	1958		Junior	R	1951	Robinson, G. W.	,,	R	1948
	,,	18	1960	Pink, E. T.	,,	14	1948		,,	20	1949
	,,	3	1961		,,	10	1949	Rodda, L. G.	,,	37	1961
Nichol, F.	,,	R	1930		Senior	13	1949	Romaine, P.	,,	4	1949
Nichol, R.	Senior	60	1965	Pope, M. W.	Junior	26	1965		Senior	6	1949
Nott, R. R.	Junior	41	1968	Porter, A. A.	,,	28	1968	Rudge, R. H.	Junior	30	1948
Nutter, J. T.	,,	21	1958	Porter, R. W.	Senior	34	1951	Rutherford, F. A.	,,	R	1953
	,,	26	1959		Junior	27	1952		Senior	R	1953
	Senior	30	1959		Senior	36	1952		Junior	26	1954
	Junior	13	1960	Potts, H. Y.	—	14	1924		Senior	9	1954
	Senior	R	1960	Potts, J. W.	Senior	R	1929		Junior	R	1955
	Junior	11	1961		Junior	R	1930		,,	12	1957
	,,	11	1962	Pratt, D.	Jnr(N)	1	1957		,,	12	1959
Oldfield, W. R.	,,	16	1954		Junior	14	1957	Rutherford, L. S.	,,	47	1955
	Senior	R	1954	Price, C. A.	,,	R	1960		Senior	R	1955
	Junior	15	1955		,,	R	1961		Junior	21	1956
	Senior	R	1955	Price, G. G.	,,	R	1960		Senior	R	1956
Ollerenshaw, H. J.	,,	46	1951	Price, N. J.	,,	R	1960	Salt, G. T.	Junior	14	1953
	Junior	50	1952		,,	R	1961		Senior	23	1953
Osborne, N.	,,	58	1949	Prince, K. R. E.	,,	21	1962	Saward, G.	Junior	28	1959
Oswin, A. T.	,,	38	1967		Senior	30	1962	Sawford, W. J.	,,	37	1956
	,,	44	1968	Purslow, C. C.	—	R	1927		,,	R	1958
Packer, C. F.	,,	R	1958	Rae, R. C.	Junior	R	1963	Scott, W.	,,	13	1964
Palmer, G.	Jnr(N)	39	1957	Rae, W.	,,	38	1959		,,	14	1965
	Junior	16	1961	Ratcliffe, K.	,,	54	1951		,,	R	1967
	,,	34	1962	Rawlings, A. W.	Senior	54	1959	Senior, G.	,,	R	1960
Pantall, G. C.	,,	11	1965	Rayner, H. W.	Junior	54	1959	Sharp, T. R. D.	,,	50	1961
	,,	R	1967		,,	32	1960		,,	54	1962
	,,	2	1968		,,	29	1962		,,	59	1963
Pantlin, E.	,,	35	1951	Raynor, A.	,,	49	1951	Sheene, F.	,,	44	1955
	,,	18	1952		,,	53	1958		Senior	44	1955
Parkinson, J.	Jnr(N)	R	1957		Senior	52	1958		Junior	51	1956
Parkinson, R. F.	—	R	1925	Redman, F.	Junior	R	1957		Senior	50	1956
	—	R	1926		Senior	R	1957	Sherry, R. H.	Junior	14	1949
Payne, K. A.	Jnr(SN)	18	1958	Rees, E.	Junior	R	1952		,,	R	1950
	Junior	R	1958		Senior	29	1952		,,	1	1951
	Senior	R	1960	Reid, G. G.	Junior	R	1965	Short, G. M.	,,	36	1967
	Junior	R	1951	Reid, J. S.	,,	R	1937		,,	17	1968
Peacock, T. G. J.	,,	53	1963	Reilly, V.	Senior	46	1958	Shortland, K. A.	,,	R	1967
Peck, R.	,,	49	1965		Junior	52	1958		,,	35	1968
Pendreigh, N. L.	,,	21	1968	Rensen, R. B.	,,	14	1951	Simister, P.	,,	24	1950
Penfold, B. E.	,,	29	1968		Senior	R	1954		Senior	31	1950
Pennington, J. S.	,,	58	1955	Reynolds, F.	Junior	R	1960	Skerritt, W.	Junior	R	1951
	Senior	R	1955		Senior	15	1960	Slade, P. R.	,,	R	1961
	Junior	R	1956		Junior	1	1961		,,	59	1962
Penton, H. R.	,,	R	1950	Reynolds, H. R.	,,	62	1960		,,	R	1964
	Senior	21	1950		,,	52	1964		,,	R	1965
Perry, D. L. F.	Junior	R	1953	Reynolds, J. C.	—	R	1927		,,	78	1959
	,,	R	1954	Rhodes, I.	Junior	37	1955	Smith, D. R.	,,	R	1960
	,,	R	1955		Senior	38	1955		Jnr(N)	14	1958
	,,	R	1957	Rice, J. M.	Junior	61	1963	Smith, D. W.	Junior	36	1958
Phillips, P. L.	,,	R	1948		,,	R	1965	Smith, J.	,,	R	1961
Phillipson, T. H.	Junior	59	1955	Richards, B.	,,	20	1962	Smith, John	,,	24	1949
	Senior	56	1955	Richardson, M.	Junior	R	1952		,,	R	1950
	Junior	R	1956		Senior	R	1952		,,	22	1951
	Senior	38	1956	Richardson, P. E.	Junior	R	1959		,,	47	1952
	Junior	16	1957	Rickard, K.	,,	R	1950	Smits, J. C.	Jnr(SN)	32	1958
	Senior	42	1957	Ritchie, R. C.	,,	9	1952		Senior	R	1958
Pike, L.	Junior	R	1933		Senior	11	1952	Staley, C. E.	Junior	11	1952
	,,	22	1937		Junior	4	1953	Standing, R. S.	,,	R	1963
Pilling, D.	Jnr(SN)	46	1958		,,	8	1957	Standivan, R. J.	,,	48	1952
	Junior	61	1959		,,	6	1958		,,	35	1953
	,,	43	1960		,,	3	1959		,,	36	1954
	,,	R	1962		,,	6	1960	Starr, L.	,,	R	1948

Name	Class	No.	Year
Starr, L.	Junior	R	1949
	Senior	39	1949
Steele, R. N.	Junior	27	1964
	„	R	1965
Stenning, B. A.	„	R	1967
	„	R	1968
Stephen, H. L.	„	7	1950
Stevens, C. A.	„	7	1948
Stevenson, J. R.	„	R	1965
Storer, N. H.	„	R	1954
Storr, D. A.	„	R	1950
	„	63	1951
	„	52	1952
Stranger, W. L.	„	R	1931
	Senior	5	1931
Stretch, R.	Junior	31	1956
	Senior	41	1956
	Junior	13	1957
	Senior	R	1957
Stringer, G. F.	Junior	50	1967
Sugden, J. A.	„	17	1960
Sutcliffe, R. B.	„	29	1967
	„	9	1968
Swales, B.	„	34	1965
Swarbrick, T. W.	Senior	23	1950
	Junior	8	1951
	Senior	R	1951
Swetman, B. J.	Junior	53	1956
	Senior	R	1956
	Junior	R	1957
	Senior	46	1957
	Junior	24	1958
	Senior	28	1958
Taylor, A. C.	Junior	30	1950
	Senior	27	1950
Taylor, C. W.	Junior	R	1968
Taylor, J. R.	„	48	1965
Taylor, R. L.	„	R	1961
	„	57	1962
	„	R	1963
	„	R	1964
Tedham, P.	„	13	1938
Templeton, M.	„	R	1950
Thompson, B. J.	„	24	1951
	„	16	1952
	„	10	1953
	„	11	1954
	„	R	1955
	„	18	1956
Thorp, T.	„	19	1956
	Senior	23	1956
Thurgood, A. J.	Junior	18	1961
Tilley, K. G.	„	R	1968
Toher, A. A. P.	„	21	1950
Tonkin, J. N.	Junior	32	1964
Trustham, J. S.	„	39	1953
	„	R	1954
	„	51	1955
	Senior	R	1955
	Junior	R	1956
	Senior	R	1956
	Junior	R	1957
	Senior	31	1957
	Junior	R	1961
Tuck, H. G. F.	Senior	54	1950
	Junior	R	1954
Tucker, A. V.	„	50	1968
Turk, A. C. T.	„	12	1951
Turner, G. H.	Senior	R	1958
	Junior	R	1959
Tyack, P. H.	Jnr(SN)	30	1958
	Senior	47	1958
	Junior	R	1964
Tynan, D.	„	44	1951
	Senior	43	1951
Uphill, M.	Junior	2	1964
	„	1	1965
Urquhart, H. L.	Jnr(SN)	17	1958
	Junior	34	1958
	„	30	1959
Varlow, J. M.	„	56	1948
	„	34	1949
	Senior	R	1949
Vivian, A. H.	Jnr(N)	R	1957
Voice, H. A.	Junior	14	1955
	Senior	15	1955
	Junior	R	1957
	Senior	54	1957
Waddington, K. D.	Junior	36	1950
	Senior	50	1950
	Junior	15	1952
Wall, H.	Senior	34	1950
Waller, J. W.	Jnr(SN)	58	1958
	Junior	74	1958
Walmsley, B.	„	R	1962
Walters, E.	„	42	1950
Walters, J. R.	„	R	1953
Ward, C. E.	„	R	1961
Warner, A. M.	„	R	1968
Warren, N. R.	„	17	1963
	„	R	1964
	„	2	1965
Warren, R. N.	„	2	1967
Washer, E. J.	„	17	1955
	Senior	24	1955
	Junior	9	1956
Wassell, M.	„	44	1957
	Senior	40	1957
Wertell, F.	Junior	68	1951
	Senior	53	1951
Watson, C. O.	Junior	R	1961
Whelan, D.	„	28	1950
	Senior	37	1950
Whiteside, A.	Junior	34	1961
Whiteside, E.	Jnr(N)	5	1957
	Junior	R	1957
	„	R	1958
Whittaker, H.	„	R	1948
Whittingham, D. J. P.	„	12	1931
Wilcox, M.	„	37	1951
	„	R	1952
	„	56	1952
Wilde, L. J.	„	R	1953
	„	46	1954
Wilkins, D. J. P.	Senior	46	1950
Willatts, R.	Junior	R	1961
	„	38	1962
Willerton, A. F.	„	R	1957
Williams, D.	„	8	1959
	Senior	17	1959
	Junior	20	1960
	„	R	1963
Williams, H. E.	„	32	1963
	„	22	1964
Williams, V. T.	„	35	1952
	Senior	R	1952
	Junior	7	1955
Willis, K.	„	29	1952
	Senior	27	1952
Wilson, J.	Jnr(N)	45	1958
Winchester, B. A.	Junior	R	1961
	„	R	1962
	„	65	1963
	„	R	1964
	„	54	1965
Winter, N.	„	R	1965
	„	20	1967
	„	R	1968
	„	66	1963
Wood, T.	Senior	25	1964
	Junior	16	1965
Wooder, E. F.	„	R	1952
Woodman, D.	„	10	1961
Wright, D.	—	R	1923
Young, L. P.	Junior	71	1955
	„	55	1956
	Senior	49	1956
	Junior	21	1957
Young, N. V.	Senior	44	1951
Young, W.	Junior	R	1960

Index